If we act now with realism and foresight,
if we show courage, if we think globally and allocate our resources accordingly,
we can give our children a more peaceful and equitable world.
One where poverty and suffering will be reduced. Where children everywhere
will have a sense of hope.
This is not just a dream. It is our responsibility.

JAMES D. WOLFENSOHN

OUR DREAM

A World Free of Poverty

SANDRA GRANZOW

FOREWORD BY JAMES D. WOLFENSOHN
PREFACE BY JAMIL SOPHER AND THIERRY BRUN
INTRODUCTION BY MICHAEL WALTON

PUBLISHED FOR
THE WORLD BANK AND WORLD BANK GROUP STAFF ASSOCIATION
OXFORD UNIVERSITY PRESS

Published by Oxford University Press, Inc.
200 Madison Avenue, New York, N.Y. 10016 U.S.A.

World Bank production and editorial assistance: Njeri Kamau and Naye Bathily

Opening photographs: Front jacket, Vietnam. Page 2, children from El Salvador. Opposite, images from the World Bank photo library.

A MEADOWS PRESS BOOK
Produced by Meadows Design Office Incorporated, Washington, D.C.
www.mdomedia.com

Creative Director and Designer: Marc Alain Meadows
Graphic Design Assistant: Heather Connelly

LIBRARY OF CONGRESS CATALOGING-IN-PUBLICATION DATA
Granzow. Sandra.
Our dream : a world free of poverty / Sandra Granzow ; foreword by James D. Wolfensohn ; preface by Jamil Sopher and Thierry Brun ; introduction by Michael Walton.
p. cm.
"A Meadows Press book"—T.p. verso.
Includes bibliographical references (p.   ) and index.
ISBN 0-19-521604-0
1. Economic assistance—Developing countries—Case studies. 2. Technical assistance—Developing countries—Case studies. 3. Poverty—Developing countries—Case studies. 4. World Bank—Developing countries—Case studies.
I. Title.
HC60.G649 2000
338.9′009172′4—dc21   00-028329

Printed and bound in China

Contents

LAND, FARMS, AND ROADS

REFORMING SCHOOLS, ENROLLING CHILDREN

THE STAFF OF LIFE

Foreword

JAMES D. WOLFENSOHN, PRESIDENT OF THE WORLD BANK GROUP

Poverty amidst plenty is the world's greatest challenge, and we at the Bank have made it our mission to fight poverty with passion and professionalism. This objective is at the center of all of the work we do, and we have recognized that successful development requires a steadily broadening and properly integrated development mandate. There is much to celebrate as we begin this new millennium. Life expectancy has risen more over the past 40 years than in the past 4,000, and democracy has spread to millions of people. But, in the midst of great wealth and a technological revolution, deep poverty persists. More than a billion people still live on less than a dollar a day, and almost three billion live on less than $2 a day. One and a half billion people still lack access to safe water, and 125 million children around the world do not attend primary school. And millions, especially children, go to bed hungry every night.

In an effort to better understand the nature and causes of poverty, we recently asked the poor about their experience with poverty in our study of 60,000 people in 60 countries. We've learned that the poor lack access to basic assets such as physical and human capital. They lack the opportunity to convert their enormous energy and hard work into a higher standard of living, and they systematically suffer from lack of influence and voice.

James D. Wolfensohn, president, World Bank Group, at a health center in Bamako, Mali.

8

These findings make us increasingly aware of the need to rethink our approach to development. Of course, economic growth and sound macroeconomic policies are critical to poverty reduction, but growth alone is insufficient. Effective poverty reduction requires sound and pro-poor institutions, effective governance, and action to deal with high levels of inequality in assets such as land and education. Poverty reduction also requires effective safety nets to mitigate the impact of personal and national calamities. And it necessitates actions to confront problems of gender and ethnic discrimination. To ensure that the benefits of growth are shared by all, both government commitment and community initiative are essential.

This book gives examples of the World Bank's work with countries at the national and local levels, in rural areas, and in cities. I am humbled by the villagers, slum dwellers, local project managers, government officials, nongovernment organizations, Bank staff, and other partners in these stories. With courage and modesty, they have made a contribution to reducing poverty. What do the stories say? That better health, well-being, and safety are possible for the poor. That people can take advantage of economic opportunities. That women can obtain an education and skills and support themselves.

Many of the stories exemplify the progress that communities can make when they become the genuine agents of development,

working together to create small businesses, improve nutrition and child care, reduce violence, and build infrastructure. Such local doers, upon gaining control of decisions and resources, often can increase the level of transparency and fair play.

With international support, national and local involvement can have a real impact. But the World Bank is only one among many actors. For this reason, we have launched a major new initiative with our partners to support country-owned poverty reduction strategies in low-income countries with the citizens, governments, and international agencies assisting them and to back these strategies with debt relief, development aid, and capacity building.

If prosperous people and nations act with realism and foresight, we can be of real help in unleashing the energies of millions of people for their own well-being. This is not just a dream; it is our responsibility.

Preface

JAMIL SOPHER, CHAIR, WORLD BANK GROUP STAFF ASSOCIATION, 1998—99
THIERRY BRUN, CHAIR, STAFF ASSOCIATION WORKING GROUP
ON POVERTY REDUCTION

The World Bank Group Staff Association is proud to join the Bank's Poverty Reduction and Economic Management Network in presenting this volume, which vividly illustrates our staff's commitment to the mission of our institution: to fight poverty with passion and professionalism for lasting results. This book tells two stories. The first story is about innovative investments, which are designed to provide public agencies, civil society, and communities with the means to stimulate economic activity or address social issues for the benefit of the poor and disenfranchised. The activities covered in this book are all producing results in alleviating poverty. They are a sampling of the many contributions to poverty alleviation being attempted by our institution and our staff.

The second story is about people. The World Bank Group staff are intensely involved, doing whatever they can to improve the condition of the weakest and most vulnerable people in the world's poorest countries. But this book also tells about leaders of government, civil society, and community groups who have shown great courage in carrying out difficult and controversial programs for the betterment of their less fortunate neighbors. And the book tells about the people who receive the benefits of World Bank Group

Those of us who have had close contact with acute poverty, famine, and the aftermath of war, feel immense gratitude in being able to help channel the resources of the Bank to help reduce these tragedies. And when I say resources, I include the Bank's technical expertise in so many fields, its relationships with the highest levels of government, its financial weight, and its accumulated wisdom.

—Thierry Brun

Jamil Sopher, chair of the World Bank Group Staff Association, 1998–99, (top), and Thierry Brun, chair of the Staff Association Working Group on Poverty Reduction.

funded programs, who have borne poverty with dignity and who seek to improve their lot through their own efforts.

The statistics about poverty, hunger, literacy, health, and other difficult problems remain bleak, especially for the world's poorest countries. But the people featured in this book believe that, by working and learning together, they are bringing about change. They seek a brighter future for those who have been bypassed by the bounty of modern society. And they derive hope and satisfaction from working toward that dream.

There have to be answers to the convenient feeling that poverty is hopeless. *Our Dream: A World Free of Poverty* points to some of the answers, and portrays the people who are toiling to make them a reality.

This book could not have been produced without the support of many people. A complete list is provided elsewhere. However, we would like to express special appreciation to the World Bank Group senior managers who provided budgetary support for the publication of this book. And we wish to thank Jim Wolfensohn, who has worked tirelessly to put a human face on poverty.

Introduction

MICHAEL WALTON, DIRECTOR,
WORLD BANK POVERTY REDUCTION BOARD AND
CHIEF ECONOMIST, HUMAN DEVELOPMENT NETWORK

Reducing poverty is a complex and difficult challenge. Poverty has many dimensions. It certainly involves lack of human and physical assets and inadequate material means to acquire food and other necessities. But it also means vulnerability to ill-health, drought, job loss, economic decline, violence, and societal conflict. And it often means a deep condition of disempowerment, even humiliation. The history of poverty during the past few decades is diverse: great advances in some dimensions in some regions, but stagnation, even reversals, in others. Progress requires effective public action at both the national and local levels, but this action is in turn profoundly influenced by how a society functions and by the public, private, and nongovernment institutions within a country. And action within a country is powerfully affected by international conditions.

The World Bank seeks to support countries in adapting international experience in poverty reduction to the design of national strategies and specific interventions. Although there is much that we have learned about what does and does not work in reducing poverty, understanding what will be effective in particular national and local circumstances is an ongoing quest. Are the activities producing the intended benefits, and what was their overall impact on the population? For instance, is a nutrition program improving child health; are education reforms resulting in higher enrollments; or is rural road construction having an impact on farming practices? To answer these questions it is necessary to evaluate the impact of both overall programs and specific interventions on individuals or households.

Evaluating impact is critical in developing countries. Resources are scarce and must be channeled where they can have the largest effect. Monitoring helps program managers know if programs are reaching their intended beneficiaries or if these programs are ineffective and wasteful. The knowledge gained provides critical input into the redesign of existing programs and the design of future interventions. The emphasis on monitoring and evaluation is part of the World Bank's determined focus on actual results for poor people and on continuous learning about what does and does not work in order to improve the efficacy of future advice and support.

The programs and projects presented in this book were selected by a team representing the Staff Association, the Poverty Reduction and Economic Management Network, and the External Affairs department of the World Bank. To be included, activities had to show poverty impact. Activities still under way had to hold the promise of enhancing the well-being of the poor and contain effective monitoring and evaluation mechanisms so that changes could be made along the way if needed. The country cases presented also include methods for monitoring and evaluation.

Impact is what counts. This volume not only shows that effective public action can make a difference to poverty in all its complexity, it also highlights the importance of understanding the impact of development measures on the poor.

Michael Walton, director, World Bank Poverty Reduction Board and chief economist, Human Development Network.

India

Uttar Pradesh is the quintessential India, home to Delhi, the Taj Mahal, the site of Buddha's first sermon, the mystical city of Varanasi, and to mountains as high as 25,000 feet. The state is also the country's most populous. More than 100 million peasants toil on tiny holdings, mostly under one hectare. Although most of the state's cultivable lands are fertile, about 10 percent are salty wastes called sodic lands. There are multiple reasons for this. The most important are the mineral salts and clay particles in the soils and the weather, which alternates between heavy monsoon and prolonged dry periods. Where drainage is blocked—naturally or by roads and canals—surface water accumulates and evaporates, leaving the salts. The sodium ion from the salts forms an electrochemical bond with the clay and leads to alkaline conditions that, at the extreme, are too toxic for farming. On top of the inadequate drainage, poor management of irrigation causes the water table to rise, creating conditions for more salt to move up to the surface and thus compounding the problem.

In Uttar Pradesh, sodic lands are either common barren areas or unproductive plots mainly owned by marginal farmers. In six months, the peasants can transform these wastelands of glaring white salts (left) into fertile farms. Once the farms are green and functioning, the farmers plant both traditional and nontraditional crops. Fruits, such as guava (above), cape gooseberry, and ber, bring in much-needed cash.

15

Overview

UTTAR PRADESH SODIC LANDS RECLAMATION PROJECT, 1993-2001

The project aims to reclaim salty wastelands and turn them into farms. 175,000 families, all small and marginal farmers, among them 50,000 previously landless laborers, are working together to reclaim the land. The peasants are taught to build wells and drainage and to apply gypsum and water to flush away the salts.

Total cost: US$112 million. World Bank (International Development Agency) US$55 million
Partner: The State of Uttar Pradesh

GOALS

Allocate lands and provide clear title.
Organize the farmers into water user groups, to manage the reclamation, carry out most of the labor, and maintain the land over time.
Involve women in a thrift and credit program to establish micro-businesses.

IMPACT BY 1998 (PROJECT ENDS IN 2001) *

Reclaimed almost 48,000 hectares and improved cropping intensity by 200 percent.

Benefited 85,000 poor families.

Increased average income of families on the reclaimed lands by 8,000 rupees.

Set up approximately 2,000 women's self-help groups, which put 8.6 million rupees into savings.

INDIA AT A GLANCE

Population: 979.7 million

Land area: 2,973,000 sq km

GNP: US$421.3 billion

GNP per capita: US$430

Poverty: 35% (of population below national poverty line)

Urban population: 28% of total population

Life expectancy at birth: 63 years

Infant mortality: 71 per 1,000 live births

Child malnutrition: 53% (of children under 5)

Access to safe water: 85% (of total population)

Illiteracy: 47% (of population age 15 and older)

* *See Appendix 1 for monitoring and evaluation information.*

Uttar Pradesh State has been fighting the salts since 1945. By the end of 1989, it had allotted thousands of hectares of sodic tracts to poor farmers and had reclaimed 157,000 hectares.

In 1993, to build upon and support the state's program, the World Bank launched the Uttar Pradesh Sodic Lands Reclamation Project. The target area is 69,000 hectares—upped, due to project successes, from a planned 45,000. The project is helping to turn the dirty salt pans into arable land, reinforcing institutions, and developing and teaching agricultural and reclamation technology.

Reclamation begins with an analysis of remote testing data, verified by field visits and testing of the soils. The next stage is to improve the surface drainage and bore tube wells, then neutralize the alkaline salts by spreading gypsum. Finally, the salts are flushed away with good quality ground water. While the application of gypsum is expensive, crops can be grown and harvested within six months of the start of the reclamation work. To prevent the salts from reinvading, the farmers must keep the land planted. Small areas of salt may appear from time to time; but with improved income from the refreshed lands, the farmers can afford to treat these spots.

LAND RECLAIMED, LIFE REBORN.
The secret lies in drainage, wells, gypsum and water, and farmers' groups that make all the decisions and do virtually all of the work.

WHO BENEFITS

About 175,000 families, all small and marginal farmers, are working together to reclaim their lands. Among them are 50,000 previously landless laborers. The small holders are gaining clear title and, with help from the project, are making their barren plots productive. As a further boost to family income, women's groups draw upon a thrift and credit program to establish micro-businesses.

HOW IT WORKS: ORGANIZING, PARTICIPATING, AND LEARNING

With the Uttar Pradesh Land Development Corporation as administrator, local nongovernment organizations pull the farmers together into water user groups. Each water user group has the responsibility of reclaiming and managing plots of four to five hectares surrounding a shallow tube well. The groups are trained to make decisions from the earliest stages and assume responsibility for all site activities, money management and accounting, maintenance of the pump sets and field and link drains, and participation in a village forum. The forum has the responsibility of allocating physical and financial resources, resolving conflicts, and monitoring the projects. The farmers provide most of the arduous labor, much of it by hand: testing, constructing the drains, applying the gypsum and water, and finally planting.

BENEFICIARIES ON EXPOSURE VISIT. *By visiting each others' villages (above left) and holding field days, the farmers learn from one another. The project also finances production of publicity materials and closely integrates the use of mass communication techniques with regular visits of field workers.*

ALLOTTING LAND. *The project staff work with the farmers to divide the land into parcels (above) and go through the sometimes complex process of ensuring clear title. Clear titles are one of the most valuable aspects of the project. In the past, it was almost impossible for the peasants to obtain them.*

IMPROVING SURFACE DRAINAGE.

After leveling the land and preparing the fields, the farmers build drains and irrigation channels. Surface drainage is very important for improving crop growth and removing excess water.

CHEMICALLY TREATING THE LAND.

Gypsum and ground water will leach away the salts and help to break down the clay in the earth. Here, the gypsum is brought to the fields by ox cart.

The work is ahead of target. Cropping intensity has shot up. Yields of rice and wheat are double what we expected. Land values have quadrupled and wage rates have doubled. New crops, including fruits and vegetables, mustard, sugarcane, and sunflower, are being grown. After the withdrawal of project assistance, farmers continue to cultivate the reclaimed lands. Non-project farmers are coming on their own to reclaim salt-affected lands just by getting gypsum from either the government or private agencies.

— M. Balasubramanian, task leader

HARD TO BELIEVE IT IS THE SAME PLACE. *Women transplant paddy and the desert begins to bloom (right). In a matter of just a few years, thousands of hectares have been brought under cultivation, revived, and made green. The local banks have increased credits to the poor. Thanks to the new prosperity, people stay put. Fewer trek to the city to search for off-season jobs.*

The success of this project is owed more than anything else to the motivation and participation of the farmers. They carry out the soil sampling, dig the irrigation channels, and apply the gypsum and the water. Thanks to the help of the local nonprofit partners, there is a systematic and complete approach to both the human and the technical side. And the flexible design has allowed us to make changes as lessons are learned.
— C. B. Paliwal, managing director of the Uttar Pradesh Land Development Corporation

The World Bank Board of Directors initially saw the project as high risk, especially with regard to the commitment of the government officials to the participatory process. They were also skeptical about the farming communities' ability to shoulder a lot of responsibility. But the project has been very well served by good managers—both C.P. Paliwal, the managing director of the Land Development Corporation, and D.K. Mittal, who preceded him and laid the foundation for the success of the project. In addition, the farmers' organizations have proven very effective.
—Seth Ashok, economist

Because my fields were barren, I used to go to Bhopal and Calcutta to look for work. Now, the fields need constant attention, and I don't have the time.
—Woman farmer

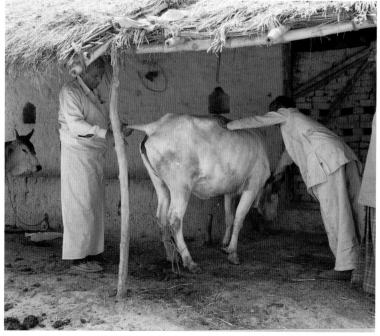

The project has helped village women (above) to organize thrift and credit organizations. The project has also brought improvements in animal husbandry (left). The boomlet in farming means work for suppliers and artisans. Micro-businesses (opposite) are burgeoning.

NEXT: ANOTHER 150,000 HECTARES

At the end of 1998, the Bank announced a US$194 million credit to continue the effort on another 150,000 hectares of sodic lands. The project model is so successful that the government of Uttar Pradesh plans to follow it in all future efforts to reclaim sodic lands.

ROOM FOR IMPROVEMENT

Despite the successes, the project organizers are concerned about the future. First, they need to find ways to reduce the cost of reclamation so the investments can be spread over even more land. Another concern is for the long-term viability of the state institutions and farmers' groups. These are indispensable to the continuing productivity of the land, and the project is doing everything possible to reinforce them.

PROJECT TEAM

M. Balasubramanian, task leader. Ridwan Ali, N. K. Bandyopadhyay, Michael Baxter, Hamdy Eisa, E.V. Jagannathan, S. Krishnan, Manoshi Mitra, Ridley Nelson, S. Rajagopal, Sarita Rana, Rebeca Robboy, Salman Salman, S. Satish, Ashok K. Seth, Harideep Singh, Sanjay Vani, K.N. Venkataraman, Edwin Lim, country director.

GOVERNMENT OF UTTAR PRADESH PARTNERS

S.K. Agarwal, C.P. Agrawal, P. Agrawal, A.Q. Alwi, C. Anant Rao, A. Dhaka, S.P. Dikshit, M. Gautam, H.C. Gupta, R.K. Gupta, Alok Jain, S.U. Khan, Raj Kumar, D.K. Mittal, I.C. Nagar, C.B. Paliwal, S. Pathak, R.S. Rao, R. S. Saxena S. Saxena, S. Srivastava, M.K. Srivastava, A.K. Tewari, A. Tripathi, D.K. Tyagi. Many others from the Remote Sensing Applications Center, the Irrigation Department, the Uttar Pradesh Council for Agriculture Research, the Ground Water Board, the Indian Institute of Management, the National Botanical Research Institute and the nonprofit organizations.

In addition to the reclamation activities, the project helps form women's savings and credit groups to supplement family incomes. These groups have become important centers of village economic activity. Banks have begun to offer the groups credits for dairy farming, sewing, tree nurseries, and trading. Some groups have even lent their savings to the menfolk to meet crop production costs. Loan repayments have been prompt, and arrears are negligible. The women's groups are so successful that the men are beginning to copy them.
— Suryanarayan Satish, social development specialist

Morocco

THE DIFFERENCE A ROAD MAKES

As you thread the narrow streets of a Moroccan town, bustling as it was in the 9th century, history comes to life—of a civilization going back as far as 500 BC and of dynasties that twice conquered most of Spain. Then, departing from the old quarter, you begin to experience an explosion of the new. You notice entire towns being built from scratch, little schools dotting the countryside, and miles and miles of irrigation ditches.

Thanks to money from emigrants and tourists, profits from phosphate, and a stable government, in 1999 the signs of Moroccan modernization were palpable. The government has been able to engineer growth through rigorous stabilization and good debt management. Gross national product per capita is around US$1,250 per year. But a huge disparity between rural and urban prosperity draws people to the cities, even though jobs there are scarce.

In the countryside, old farming methods, low-value crops, and patchy health care and schooling keep many Moroccans mired in poverty. Thus, there is an urgent need for vigorous growth.

Where the road ends (above) ancient life persists—picturesque but arduous. The truck has gone as far as it can. Its cargo will be unloaded onto the strong backs of donkeys and people. The oldest mode of conveyance (right). In the remote mountains of Morocco, the human foot can find the way on the stoniest of paths. In such isolated areas, cash crops are limited to produce that won't spoil during the long trip to market.

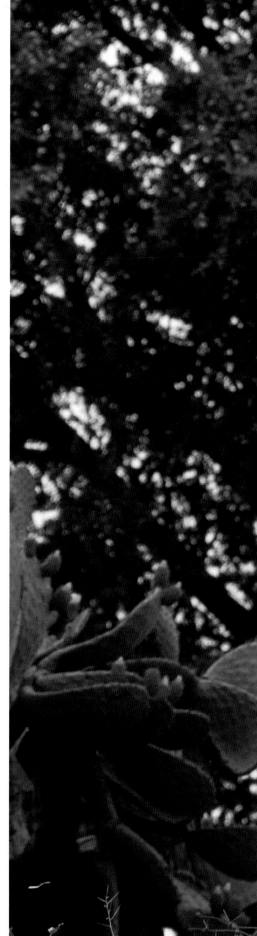

… Watch the little caravan … on its way home to the next village, to those rock-colored houses that cling to the side of the hill and seem to be watching you, crouching behind their rampart of cactus. This path here leads to the spring. Women come away from it, bent under the weight of heavy jars and red earthenware… The road is long…. At last the weary traveler sees, outlining itself against the gray-mauve of the sky, the indistinct silhouette of a minaret.

— Ahmed Sefrioui, Morocco, 1956

Overview

FOURTH HIGHWAY PROJECT, 1984-90

Total project cost: US$131 million (World Bank: US$85 million)
Rural road components: US$24 (construction and improvement of about 575 km)

EMERGENCY DROUGHT RECOVERY PROJECT, 1995-98

Total project cost: US$334 million (World Bank: US$96 million)
Rural road components: US$85 million (construction and improvement of about 1,650 km)

SECONDARY, TERTIARY, AND RURAL ROADS PROJECT, 1996-2001

Total project cost: US$194 million (World Bank: US$58 million)
Rural road components: US$32 million (construction and improvement of about 1,235 km)

GOALS

Improve access to markets, agricultural extension, health care, education, and other services. Reduce the costs of essential goods, such as fuel and agricultural inputs.

IMAPCT IN FOUR AREAS IN 1995 *

Share-ride taxis run approximately every hour, compared with sporadic bus service.
Firewood hauled on foot has been replaced with low-cost butane, delivered by truck.
Girls' enrollment in school trebled to 40%; overall enrollment doubled.
Small farm use of extension services quadrupled; dairy yield doubled; fruit orchard yields improved by almost one-third.

MOROCCO AT A GLANCE

Population: 27.8 million

Land area: 446,000 sq km

GNP: US$34.8 billion

GNP per capita: US$1,250

Poverty: 13% (percent of population below national poverty line)

Urban population: 54% of total population

Life expectancy at birth: 67 years

Infant mortality: 51 per 1,000 live births

Child malnutrition: 10% (of children under 5)

Access to safe water: 57% of population

Illiteracy: 54% (of population age 15 and older)

* See Appendix 1 for monitoring and evaluation information.

The country has taken aim at its poverty. The government has started investing heavily in irrigated agriculture and better crops, food self-sufficiency, health, and education. Roads, the focus of this chapter, form the armature for these services, which seek to help the rural population prosper and reduce income disparities between regions.

For the foreign visitor to the rural areas of countries such as Morocco, one of the chief attractions is the absence of the material junk and blandness that seem to accompany development. Any backpacker who has trekked the roadless byways of the developing world becomes attached to the unspoiled isolation, but also concerned about the poverty. It is unpleasant to recognize that what charms the visitor sometimes severely taxes the inhabitants, especially the women.

The track from Targa N'Touchka Village continues through miles and miles of stone and scrub.

In the remote mountains of the north, a woman (left) lies down on the stack of wood she has gathered and attaches a rope. Her daughter helps her get up. It is six in the morning, but she must cook breakfast for her six children and her epileptic husband. Carrying firewood is the daily chore of all the poor women living here in the mountain enclaves of the north. They can't afford gas. Transportation on long, rocky trails would make the cost prohibitive.

Trudging home—two to three kilometers—is arduous. The woman carries about 50 to 60 kg—almost an entire tree, plus her baby. She forages for wood three times a day. On her last trip today, she will carry 30 kg, which is not enough, according to her.

What difference does a road make? What happens to people? Their
farms? Their lives? In 1996, the World Bank Operations Evaluation
Department asked these questions of people living along rural
roads in several distinct Moroccan regions, each with different soils,
rainfall patterns, and economies.

The four roads under study were among 10 that were from 30 to
50 km long, which previously had been gravel or unimproved track
with traffic volumes generally below 100 vehicles per day. During
the course of the World Bank's Fourth Highway Project (1983–90),
these roads were paved, with dramatic results.

ACCESS TO SERVICES, THE MARKET,
AND HEALTH CARE. *The bus (right)
travels the link between Barrage
Moulay Youssf and DTamouda. The
road brought lower prices for household goods and agricultural inputs
and saved people hours and hours of
walking. In some cases, the time to
reach county and village administrative offices, agricultural extension
personnel, health centers, and rural
markets was cut in half. In one town,
the number of kiosks in the weekly
market shot up from 10 to more than
500. Visits to health care facilities
nearly doubled.*

In a region still without a paved road, Mrs. Naciri (below) carries her sick three-year-old many miles to the doctor. Two years ago in Fifi, after the road came, a hospital was built and with it came ambulance service (left).

Year-round traffic became a norm. Road closures went down from 90 days to zero. The greater accessibility and lower vehicle operating costs transformed the economy.
—Hernan Levy, coordinator-transport cluster, Operations Evaluation Department

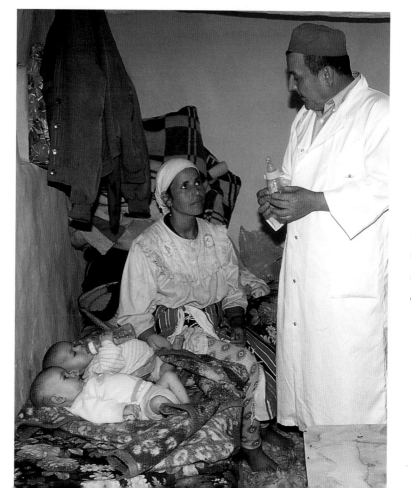

For 33 years, Mr. Bekkali, left, has worked in Fifi for the Ministry of Health treating numerous and mortal illnesses: meningitis, typhoid, malaria, leprosy. In the past, arriving at the invalid's home after a long trip on foot or mule, Mr. Bekkali could usually offer little more than to share the tears of the family. Now, thanks to the road, he can easily visit his patients. He has records of all the births. All the children in his area are vaccinated. Here at left, he visits the seven-month-old twins of farmer Mohamed Alami.

In the past, I couldn't afford fertilizer. The trip from the market cost 60DH for myself and 120DH for the sack— more than the fertilizer cost. Now I pay 5DH for my one-hour ride, and some of the merchants deliver the fertilizer for free. With fertilizer, I can get much better yields, and again thanks to the road, I can quickly get my produce to market.

— The son of Mr. Ouled Samka, farmer, sprinkling fertilizer on his crop.

Thanks to drops in cost and the ease of transport, fertilizer use has leapt by more than 60 percent in two of the areas that were studied.

Farmers have shifted production to high-value fruits and vegetables. Perishable produce can get quickly to market. Farmers' use of agricultural extension services has quadrupled and brought better farming techniques. Access to irrigation equipment and improved seeds has made a dramatic difference. The changes have brought greater prosperity. And, with the availability of fish, fruit, and vegetables, diets have improved.

The roads have saved women two to three hours a day of precious time previously spent collecting firewood. The switch to butane has reduced the pressure on the country's scarce forests. At left, a helper lifts a tank of butane onto a shared-ride van, which will carry the farmers and their merchandise home from market.

*In Morocco, the government has established a road maintenance fund, which receives revenues from gasoline taxes. The fund is being used to improve and expand the rural road network. The fund is supplemented by yearly allocations from Morocco's general budget and by the World Bank's loans. In addition, rural governments and communities are expected to co-finance around 12 percent of their local roads. This cost sharing helps to get the roads built and ensure local commitment to and oversight of regular maintenance.
— Mohammed Feghoul, highway engineer*

By 1995, Morocco had 57,500 kilometers of road. About half were paved. But 40 percent were in bad condition and a quarter were impassable during bad weather. One-fifth of the country's villages remained totally isolated, inaccessible by vehicle.

The government and the World Bank continue to see roads as critical for development. A government commitment to improve or pave another 15,000 kilometers is well under way. That's a lot of road—more than three times the distance across the United States.

The weather has a habit of sabotaging the best of human intentions. In 1994–95, a drought reduced Morocco's agricultural gross domestic product by 45 percent. Heavy rains in 1995–96 brought a quick recovery of harvests and replenishment of aquifers and man-made reservoirs. But, for a number of months, the already poor rural areas were struck very hard.

Consistent with the government's strategic plan and in record time, the World Bank responded with the Emergency Drought Recovery Project. The project brought assistance in agriculture and drinking water and supported the construction and rehabilitation of 1,650 kilometers of rural roads. The project was completed in three years and was rated highly satisfactory by the Bank's Operations Evaluation Department.

The Bank is financing another 1,235 kilometers of rural roads under the Secondary, Tertiary, and Rural Roads Project (1996–2001).

Children walk home from school on the road from Barrage Moulay Youssf to DTamouda, opposite. The government has constructed schools and other services along the roads. Teachers and other professionals are willing to travel to jobs whereas, in the past, the remoteness was a deterrent.

One of the most spectacular results has been the tripling of girls' school enrollment. The proximity of the schools, the ease of transportation, and the greater safety from attacks on lonely paths have all played a part in this change.

Overall school attendance has increased. Primary school enrollment in 1995 reached 68 percent, compared with 28 percent in 1985. The enhanced roads made the schools more attractive to students as well as teachers.

In 1994–95, Morocco was struck by drought. The government took imme-diate and thoughtful action to maintain the lifelines of agriculture, drinking water, and roads so that food could get to market and farmers could purchase animal feed and cereal seeds. The World Bank helped with a drought recovery loan, part of which was directed to rehabilitating and building additional rural roads.
— Trayambkeshwar Sinha,
task team leader, Emergency Drought Recovery Project

Low volume, narrow paved roads in rural Morocco cost $100,000 per kilometer, while gravel roads cost $20,000 per kilometer. For the same investment budget, you can thus construct five times more gravel roads than paved ones. And reach five times more people. The trade-off is that it costs more to operate a vehicle on gravel roads and they are less comfortable to drive on. They also will quickly revert to a terrible state if they are not maintained. Morocco's rural road needs are large. While not popular, gravel is a necessary evil until traffic picks up. In the newer projects, where traffic is light and gravel is available locally at a low price, gravel has been used extensively.
— Jaffar Bentchikou, principal highway engineer

THE COMING CHALLENGE

There are two sides to Morocco: the rich modern, urban side and the neglected, poor rural side. Roads are helping to change the balance, and so are the schools, clinics, and other services which are being put into place along the roads. But there remain deep social disparities and a need for jobs, which can be met as Morocco moves further toward a truly modern economy.

PROJECT TEAM

Mohammed Feghoul, task team leader, Secondary, Tertiary and Rural Roads Project. Trayambkeshwar Sinha, task team leader, Emergency Drought Recovery Project. Hernan Levy, OED evaluation team leader. Henri Beenhakker, Jaffar Bentchikou, J. Benzekri, Adel Bichara, Abdeljalil Bounhar, M. Bounouar, K. Ghellab, Janati Idrissi, A. Imzel, Majid Kettani, Karim Laraki, Linda Likar, Michel A. Loir, James Lowenthal, Brigitte Meline, Klaus Mersman, Driss Meski, A. R'mili, Isabelle Tsakok, Claudine Voyadzis. Christiane Delvoie, country director.

Morocco has a new king, Mohammed VI, who came to the throne in July 1999, after the death of his father, King Hassan II. King Mohammed VI has indicated that he will emphasize, among other programs, schools and jobs for both urban and rural citizens. The king's goal is to build a country that will forge close links with the European Union and with other Mediterranean countries. The coalition government he inherited represents the spectrum of views in Morocco, and the head of it is a socialist leader who at one time was one of the country's most prominent political dissidents. If the king continues Morocco's trend toward a more representative system of government, with the support of a growing modern, dynamic and outward looking segment of society, he may be the catalyst for Morocco to realize the advantages of its talents and culture and of its geographic position near Europe.
— Paolo Zacchia,
Morocco country economist

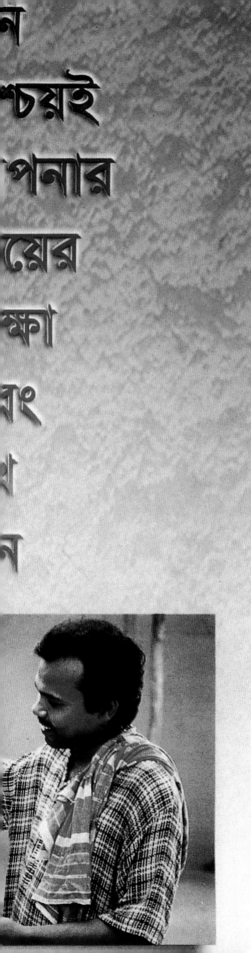

Bangladesh

AN EDUCATION FOR KULSUM

Laced with rivers and lush with tea plantations and tropical vegetation, Bangladesh is home to the Bengal tiger, monkeys, gibbons, crocodiles and a myriad of other species. But the country is also the most densely populated in the world and is growing, fast. Its 123 million people are plagued by annual floods, hurricanes, and extreme poverty. Nine out of ten children are to some degree malnourished. Since separating from Pakistan in 1971, Bangladesh has invested heavily in human development. Although economic growth has been too slow to reduce poverty, some of these investments are beginning to pay off. Key social indicators—birth rates, life expectancy, and child immunization—have improved remarkably.

GIRLS: A RESOURCE FOR FAMILY AND NATION

As recently as 1991, the educational attainment of Bangladeshi women was among the lowest in the world. Eighty percent were illiterate. Equipped with few skills and ignorant about health care, family planning, and nutrition, they were trapped in a cycle of dependency.

Bangladeshi culture once seemed to guarantee that girls would marry young and receive little education. But times are changing. Economic pressures and the departure of many men for jobs abroad,

"You must be caring for your daughters' education," says this poster in the Bangla language (opposite). *"The days of unhappiness are over. The government will help you defray the education expenses."* The fate of Bangladeshi girls lies with their fathers, who are the family decision makers. Any effort to change women's lives must begin by influencing fathers.

39

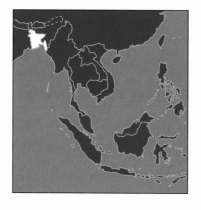

Where the mind is

without fear and

the head is held high,

Where knowledge is

free . . .

Into that heaven of

freedom, my Father,

let my country awake.

—from "Geetanjali" by Rabindranath Tagore. (Tagore wrote India's national anthem but was born in what is now Bangladesh. Both countries claim him as one of their greatest poets.)

Overview

FEMALE SECONDARY SCHOOL ASSISTANCE PROJECT

The project provides stipends to approximately 1 million girls to cover tuition, transportation, uniforms, sports, school supplies, examination fees, and other expenses. The program includes occupational training and health education and funds the building of school latrines.

Total financing: US$88.4 million

Bank Group contribution: US$68 million (International Development Agency)

GOALS

Increase the number of girls enrolled in grades six to ten and help them to pass their Secondary School Certificate examinations.

Build the confidence and social status of the female.

ACHIEVEMENT*

By 1998, the number of girls enrolled in grades six to ten had grown from 238,000 to 861,000, exceeding the 1999 target.

BANGLADESH AT A GLANCE

Population: 125.6 million

Land area: 130,000 sq km

GNP: US$44 billion

GNP per capita: US$350

Poverty: 36%
(percent of population below national poverty line)

Urban population:
20% of total population

Life expectancy at birth:
58 years

Infant mortality:
75 per 1,000 live births

Child malnutrition: 56%
(of children under 5)

Access to safe water: 84%
(of total population)

Illiteracy: 61%
(of population age 15 and older)

* See Appendix 1 for monitoring and evaluation information.

coupled with the influence of dynamic nonprofit organizations engaged in social mobilization, have created a new climate.

Women are becoming active in their communities and the economy. Development programs are helping poor women start businesses, form savings and credit groups, and work for wages.

COST IS THE MAIN OBSTACLE TO SECONDARY EDUCATION

Secondary education requires tuition fees in Bangladesh. Transportation, uniforms, sports, school supplies, and examination fees are additional. And Bangladesh is so poor that even for the so-called middle class, one child's tuition can consume as much as half of the family's disposable income.

THE FEMALE SECONDARY SCHOOL ASSISTANCE PROJECT

To encourage families to educate their girls and help cover the high costs, in the early 1990s the World Bank and the government of Bangladesh set up the Female Secondary School Assistance Project. This project's goals are to increase the number of girls enrolled in the first several years of secondary school (grades six to ten) and help them to pass their secondary school certificate examinations so that they become qualified for employment.

The project aims to hold the girls in their studies, discourage them from early marriage and child bearing, and thereby slow population growth. By its nature, the project should help a new generation of women to emerge more confident and with a higher status in society.

PROJECT COMPONENTS

The project incorporates a series of components that, when combined, have changed the face of girls' education in Bangladesh: stipends to girls for expenses and to their schools for tuition (77 percent of the project's total budget); occupational training; health education, including reproductive health; water and sanitation—latrines for 3,870 schools; salaries for additional secondary teachers; recruiting of more female teachers; and parent groups and school management committees.

Across the country, a social communication program promotes girls' education. Thousands of leaflets, posters, and brochures have been distributed to promote changes in family and community values and behavior.

The program aims especially at men because its research showed that it is the fathers—often influenced by a relative or a villager, also male—who make the decision to educate their daughters.

Kulsum's story, portrayed here, comes from a brochure distributed by the Ministry of Education. Reflecting the research, the story dramatizes the parents' problems in paying, the father's prerogative as decision-maker, the influence of a male relative, and the happy outcome, thanks to the stipend paid by the program.

Kulsum, the meritorious student of Class 5, no longer goes to school. She is carrying lunch to her father who is working in the fields.

On the way, Kulsum meets her uncle. Uncle: "Kulsum, are you not going to school?" Kulsum: "No, uncle. I am going to the field, taking father's meal. I don't think I can continue with my education."

Uncle: *"What's the matter? You are the best student of Class 5. The exams are ahead. Your anxieties would be over if you crossed over to Class 6."* Kulsum: *"What are you talking about, uncle? It would be more expensive in Class 6. That means more pressure on father. That's why I stopped here. There is no way out."* Uncle: *"No, Kulsum, you are wrong. I am sure you don't know the good news. Let's go to your father. I'll tell him something surprising."*

Kulsum's father: *"Hi, Zamir. What's the matter? When did you come?"* Uncle: *"Just today. Rush to me. I have something very urgent to discuss with you regarding Kulsum's education."*

"Zamir, it's really surprising. The Government would bear expense for Kulsum's education? From Class 6 up to Class 10?"

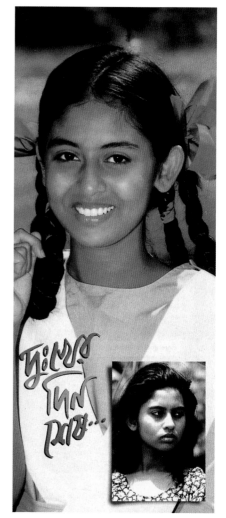

The picture story of Kulsum is told in a brochure, as well as on posters and calendars widely distributed throughout Bangladesh. Such communication tools draw from authentic situations and use gentle language—attempting to touch a father's concern for his daughter, while acknowledging and offering a solution to his practical problems. The brochure cover at right reads: "The days of unhappiness are over."

42

The Bank conducted extensive research to understand exactly why Bangladeshi girls were not staying in school. Some factors that played a role were early marriage and child bearing and poor employment opportunities for women. Also, many schools lacked reliable water sources and latrines.

The project design spoke to these issues through stipend programs, occupational skills development, and water supply and sanitation programs.

To be eligible for the stipend program, daughters must remain unmarried, attend school 75 percent of the school year, and obtain at least 50 percent marks in the final examinations. Thanks to these well-conceived incentives, girls' enrollment has risen considerably, and attitudes have changed. The supervision reports show how the families, villagers, and government have rallied around girls' education.

I think this project will have a long-lasting impact on the status of females in Bangladesh.
—Deborah Lee Ricks, team assistant

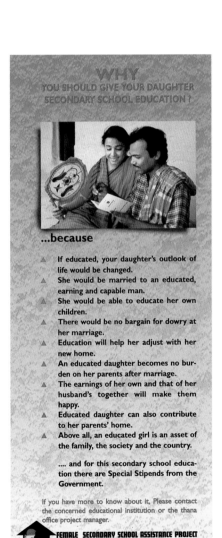

WHY
YOU SHOULD GIVE YOUR DAUGHTER
SECONDARY SCHOOL EDUCATION ?

...because

▲ If educated, your daughter's outlook of life would be changed.
▲ She would be married to an educated, earning and capable man.
▲ She would be able to educate her own children.
▲ There would be no bargain for dowry at her marriage.
▲ Education will help her adjust with her new home.
▲ An educated daughter becomes no burden on her parents after marriage.
▲ The earnings of her own and that of her husband's together will make them happy.
▲ Educated daughter can also contribute to her parents' home.
▲ Above all, an educated girl is an asset of the family, the society and the country.

.... and for this secondary school education there are Special Stipends from the Government.

If you have more to know about it, Please contact the concerned educational institution or the thana office project manager.

FEMALE SECONDARY SCHOOL ASSISTANCE PROJECT
DIRECTORATE OF SECONDARY & HIGHER EDUCATION,
MINISTRY OF EDUCATION.

HOW THE STIPENDS AND TUITION ARE DISPENSED

The Stipend Operations Manual of the Bank project is used across the country:

The project signs agreements with banks whose local branches disburse the tuition and stipends.

The local banks open an account for each girl and another account for tuition fees, which go to the schools.

An MIS system maintains and links information, based on the ID numbers given to the girls, the schools, and the banks.

The girls are given passbooks and checkbooks. They must personally make the withdrawals by writing a check.

The district project officers conduct surprise visits to review school records and evaluate the girls' attendance and performance. They are expected to discuss low performance or low attendance with guardians, parents, and teachers.

The schools are required to encourage girls to enroll and to issue warnings to girls who are falling behind in attendance or grades.

We have almost 900,000 girls now and will have 100,000 more, each with a file—name, picture, commitment to perform, grades, attendance, family situation. They are individuals, learning one-by-one, and we monitor them one-by-one. When I think of my own daughters with their fine education and privileges, I am very happy to know the project is changing the life chances of so many girls in Bangladesh.
—Ana Maria Jeria, task leader

A TRIUMPH OF NATIONAL MAGNITUDE

The Bank-supported project covers about one-quarter of the country. But, because requests for stipends have been numerous, in 1994 the government decided to expand coverage to the entire country. The Asian Development Bank and the Government of Norway are assisting with the national program.

By July 1997, the gap between girls' and boys' enrollment in the project area was virtually eliminated. Girls receiving Secondary School Certificates increased from 42 percent in 1996 to 52 percent in 1997. Equally salutary, close to 100 percent of primary-age girls are in school.

DAUNTING CHALLENGES REMAIN

Successful as the project has been, there are still problems to be resolved—and not easily:

Two-thirds of the nation's girls still cannot attend secondary school—a reality rooted in poverty. The government is now aiming to target the poorest by offering them higher stipends. However, given the poverty of the entire country, the government may have difficulty continuing the stipends. Sustainability is a matter still to be tackled.

The number of female teachers has increased but remains at around 7 percent of all new recruits. The project is redoubling efforts but the gap will be hard to close.

Limited job opportunities, intertwined with cultural restrictions, discourage women from seeking jobs. That the project cannot recruit enough female teachers is symptomatic of the low numbers of educated adult women. Only with economic development, increased job opportunities, and a continuing change in attitudes can one expect a broader impact on the lives of Bangladeshi women. The hope is that opportunities will gradually open up and that educated girls will be prepared to fill them.

The students are given passbooks and checkbooks. To obtain their stipends, they must personally write a check.

PROJECT TEAM

Ana Maria Jeria, task leader. Mir Bashir Ahmed, Milia Ali, Mohammed Allak, Irajen Appasamy, Ann Hamilton, Ralph Harbison, William Herbert, Wahida Huq, Martin Karcher, Laura Kiang, Mieko Nishimizu, Habibur Rahman, Deborah Ricks, Mohammed Sayeed, Thomas Schmidt, Tabassum Shahnaz, Nazma Sultana, Paula Valad, Cecilia Verzosa, Suraiya Zannath. Fred Temple, country director.

El Salvador

El Salvador's education reform has roots in the 1980s: While government services were at a standstill in the areas most affected by the country's civil war, many communities hired teachers with their own funds and organized classrooms in churches, shanties, or whatever space they could come by. At the close of the war, half a million mostly rural children had no access to school. To serve them, the Ministry of Education turned to the successful grassroots model of parent-run schools and, in 1991, began organizing community education associations to run schools across the countryside. With World Bank assistance, the ministry provided the funds and trained the associations. Thus began the well-known EDUCO project. By January 1999, parent associations were managing more than 6,400 EDUCO classrooms and serving 206,000 students—22 percent of the country's five- to twelve-year-olds. These schools increased enrollment, improved administration, established adult education services, and dramatically bolstered teacher attendance. The rural-focused EDUCO program was so successful that in 1996–97 the ministry took the step of expanding school-based management to the country's more than 4,000 elementary, middle and secondary schools. Though somewhat less autonomous, the local parent-teacher councils are modeled after those in the EDUCO program.

El Salvador's education reforms have placed management decisions for each school in the hands of school councils, run by parents, teachers, and principals. The Ministry of Education directs training and support to these councils. The Ministry has also expanded school facilities, boosted enrollment, revised curricula, improved teacher training and testing, and upgraded management capacity. Modern arithmetic, ancient tool (above). New curriculum, mischief as always (right).

Sowers of ideas, the people are the earth [in which you plant your seeds]. If the people are sand, rock, an ignorant mass, your hard work will be useless. First you have to fertilize and give them receptive capacity; that is to say in our case, teach them to read, habituate them to read, accustom them not only to read but to under-stand.

— Alberto Masferrer, respected Salvadoran educator

Overview

EDUCATION REFORM, 1991-2005

Long-term commitment to supporting El Salvador as it builds schools, expands enrollment, and improves the quality of teaching and materials.

GOALS

Ensure that 90 percent of El Salvador's children complete grade 9 by the year 2005.

Expand secondary schools, benefiting 134,000 students, with an emphasis on services to the poorest.

Devolve power to the school level and train parents so they can participate in management councils.

Improve teacher training.

Promote enrollment and attendance.

Deliver on-site health services and snack programs to children in the poorest schools.

TARGETS OF THE SECONDARY EDUCATION PROJECT: 1997 TO 2002 *

Increase the gross enrollment rate in secondary schools from 27 percent to 30 percent by 2004.

Increase the transition rate between 9th and 10th grades from 78 percent to 90 percent.

Significantly increase the mean achievement scores for mathematics, language and science.

EL SALVADOR AT A GLANCE

Population: 6.1 million

Land area: 21,000 sq km

GNP: US$11.2 billion

GNP per capita: US$1,850

Poverty: 48% (of population below national poverty line)

Urban population: 46% of total population

Life expectancy at birth: 69 years

Infant mortality: 32 per 1,000 live births

Child malnutrition: 11% (of children under 5)

Access to safe water: 53% (of total population)

Illiteracy: 23% (of population age 15 and older)

* See Appendix 1 for monitoring and evaluation information.

TEN-YEAR PLAN: UNIVERSAL NINTH GRADE EDUCATION

Even as community participation was improving education
services, many schools still lacked textbooks. School facilities,
teacher training, and administrative functions were sadly deficient.
In the countryside, Salvadorans over the age of 15 had completed
fewer than three years of school; in urban areas, the average was
seven years.

After broad consultation with the civil society, the Ministry of
Education designed a 10-year education plan (1995–2005), with the
goal of ensuring that at least 90 percent of El Salvador's children
complete grade 9 by the year 2005.

Funded by the World Bank and the InterAmerican Development
Bank, the basic education reforms have focused on areas with low
enrollment rates, high repetition rates, and many overage children.

*This school combines primary educa-
tion and child health services. Signage
reads: "Welcome to my healthy school,
Caserio San Pedro."*

49

In the past, most teachers and students at the elementary level had to rely on a blackboard, chalk, paper, pencils, and little else, far left. During the past few years, the Ministry of Education has completely revamped school curricula. New textbooks, left, incorporate information about El Salvador's history, culture, geography, and natural environment; eliminate sexist stereotypes; and reflect the principles of democracy.

RESULTS: DROPOUT RATE FALLS, LITERACY IMPROVES

In 1999, efforts to improve teacher training, empower parents, promote attendance, modernize procedures, and decentralize administration—all designed to support the local schools—are well under way. Among notable accomplishments, the government has helped many rural communities build new schools and renovate old ones.

There are so many unforgettable moments. You see how the ideas you've been dreaming of come true, how many people all over the country have put so much effort into making education a priority, how the parents interpret the ideas and put them into practice, how much ownership there is. It touches me very much to hear parents who think I don't know about the program trying to convince me how important it is to their lives and to their children.

— Madalena dos Santos, task manager

The elementary, middle, and secondary programs use careful targeting to be sure that schools in the neediest communities get resources. In the Salvadoran view, "Educacion es la Solucion" (education is the solution). Families believe this and are taking advantage of the improved educational opportunities: From 1989 to 1995, net enrollment in grades one through six increased from 70 percent to 88 percent. The dropout rate decreased from 15 percent to 6 percent.

Snack programs (opposite top) improve nutrition. With full stomachs, the children can enjoy school and learning.

In almost 3,600 Escuelas Saludables (healthy schools), the ministries of Education and Health collaborate to provide primary health care to more than 600,000 students (opposite bottom).

With virtually all of El Salvador's secondary schools located in urban areas, fewer than 30 percent of the country's 15- to 19-year-olds were enrolled. Rural youth were left out almost entirely. On top of this, there had been no major changes in secondary education for twenty years. Thus, the Ministry of Education and the World Bank began planning the new Secondary Education Project.

Initiated in 1998, the Secondary Education Project will benefit 134,000 students. Although targeting all secondary schools, the project maintains emphasis on the poorest. A scholarship program provides for greater equity in access and improved gender equity.

COVERAGE, QUALITY, CAPACITY

Consistent with the earlier reforms, the Secondary Education Project emphasizes—

EXTENDED COVERAGE: new or rehabilitated schools and classrooms; distance learning programs for rural students; scholarships for the most needy. Because private schools serve 52 percent of secondary school children, they are included in many of the ministry's programs.

I have day-to-day telephone contact with the top managers in the Ministry. They have such enthusiasm to get things done. They are down to earth, not pretentious. I have the utmost respect for them and for their accomplishments in education reform, and I truly enjoy the camaraderie between our team and our client.

— Julie Nannucci, program assistant

Consultation and participation are bywords. The school councils, composed of teachers, directors, parents, and students, are responsible for planning and implementing the school activities, participating in managing resources transferred to the schools, and raising additional funds. Here, a father attends training for members of the school council. He is learning about the model receipt for teacher pay: "Received from the Community Association for Basic Education...."

IMPROVED QUALITY: curriculum development; in-service teacher training; learning resource centers; achievement tests; a school accreditation system.

STRENGTHENED MANAGERIAL CAPACITY: systems to support decentralized school-based management; training for school councils; public awareness campaigns to build support for secondary education.

THE DOWNSIDE

El Salvador is not without its problems. Political disagreements have slowed implementation of education reforms. Teacher salaries are still low, government funds for education are insufficient, and the quality of teaching still needs to improve. Street gangs have proliferated and, with them, the incidence of violence. Many young people suffer from malnutrition. Teenage pregnancy and forced entry into the labor market to subsidize family incomes often cut education short. With Bank support, efforts are being made, but these are thorny, long-term issues.

TOTAL BANK LENDING

From 1991 to 2005, total Bank commitments for education in El Salvador will have been US$271 million, according to the current schedule. While the Bank's credits have been in the form of projects, the intention has been to help finance El Salvador's long-term integrated program of education reform.

PROJECT TEAM

Madalena dos Santos, task manager. Genaro Alarcon-Benito, Maria Elena Anderson, Ana Maria Arriagada, Eduardo Atalah, Jose Augusto Carvalho, Maria Correia, Yael Duthilleul, John Edwards, Rosita Estrada, Sandra Granzow, Orville Grimes, Andrea Guedes, Cynthia Hobbs, Olympia Icochea, Aurora Kirk, Theresa Lobo, Richard Moore, Julie Nannucci, Suhas Parandekar, Valeria Junho Pena, Livio Pino, Jorge Quintana, Joel Reyes, Ana-Maria Rodriguez-Ortiz, Eleanor Schreiber, Ricardo Silveira, Diane Steele, Donald Winkler, Carolyn Winter, Alfred Wood, Alberto Zuniga. Donna Dowsett-Coirolo, country director.

India

Malnutrition lacks the drama and visibility of a catastrophe, but it is a relentless killer of young children and their mothers. Malnutrition in India is worse than it is in Africa. Since the 1970s, the well-being of India's population has improved. Average life expectancy at birth has increased from 50 years to 63. The birthrate has fallen from six to three children per woman. But, with its population nearing a billion, India still has 16 million new mouths to feed every year. And more than half the children of all ages are malnourished.

Nutrition in the southeastern state of Tamil Nadu has historically been even worse than the average. In 1981, 25 of the different nutrition programs that were operating in the state cost the government about $9 million annually. Yet for various reasons, these programs reached only a fraction of the most vulnerable groups.

"The irony is that we know what to do," says Anthony Measham, public health physician and World Bank task leader. "The answers are feasible and affordable: growth monitoring, largely as a means of educating mothers about malnutrition; inexpensive micronutrients; foods rich in Vitamin A; education and behavior change among

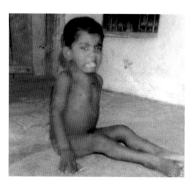

BEFORE AND AFTER. *Datshayina's legs were so weak she couldn't stand (above). She was severely malnourished and had infantile tuberculosis, worms, and anemia. But she got help. The Navlog Community Nutrition Center, part of the Tamil Nadu Nutrition Project, sent her to a rehabilitation center where she was given nutritious meals and to a local hospital for medical treatment. Now nine-year-old Datshayina (right) is the highest scorer in her class.*

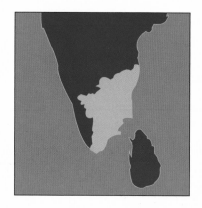

*On a greenish hill by the
name of Courtalam,
there are five waterfalls.*

*Likewise, for a mother-
to-be, there are five
things to remember.*

*Early registration,
tetanus shots, regular
weighing, iron tablets,*

And food and rest, too.

— *by Muniyammal, popular singer*

Overview

TAMIL NADU INTEGRATED NUTRITION PROJECTS, 1981-1997

A nutrition and health program based on growth monitoring, short-term supplemental feeding and teaching proper nutrition.

Total cost: US$200 million.

World Bank (International Development Agency): US$128 million.

GOALS

Monitor children's growth through periodic weighing and measuring.

Temporarily provide food to the children who are not growing on a normal trajectory.

Where needed, provide food to adolescents and pregnant women.

Mobilize and train women at the small neighborhood level so that they understand nutrition and permanently change their own eating habits as well as the way they feed their children.

IMPACT OF THE FIRST TAMIL NADU NUTRITION PROJECT DURING THE 1980S *

Reduced severe malnutrition among children six to 36 months old by 26 to 42 percent (varied with location).

Reduced infant mortality rate by 26 to 29 percent in the earlier phases of the project and by 12 to 13 percent in the later phases.

INDIA AT A GLANCE

Population: 979.7 million

Land area: 2,973,000 sq km

GNP: US$421.3 billion

GNP per capita: US$430

Poverty: 35% (of population below national poverty line)

Urban population: 28% of total population

Life expectancy at birth: 63 years

Infant mortality: 71 per 1,000 live births

Child malnutrition: 53% (of children under 5)

Access to safe water: 85% (of total population)

Illiteracy: 47% (of population age 15 and older)

* See Appendix 1 for monitoring and evaluation information.

The Tamil Nadu Intergrated Nutrition Project (TINP) represents the World Bank's long-term commitment to a huge nutrition and health program based on growth monitoring and short-term supplemental feeding. A central tenet is that most malnutrition results from inappropriate childcare practices, and not from income, famine, or unpreventable health problems, though these factors can be important.

The drawing (below left) shows monthly weighing, with the data recorded on growth charts that the mothers can easily understand.

mothers and girls; nutrition for adolescent girls, including iron tablets; and community participation."

The Integrated Nutrition Project, embarked on by the state of Tamil Nadu and the World Bank in 1981, incorporates all of these elements. Covering more than 13 million rural people, the project has been one of the most successful in the world in reducing severe malnutrition. "The single most important feature is the targeting of supplementary feeding to young, malnourished children, as identified by growth monitoring," says Dr. Measham, until recently the Bank's team leader for the project. "Programs which try to feed everyone fail."

Females have low status in Indian society. As a result, women and girls literally get less food and health care than males. Many women 'eat down' in fear of a difficult delivery caused by a large baby. A vicious cycle commences when a malnourished or ill mother gives birth to a low birth-weight female child. She remains small in stature and pelvic size due to further malnourishment, and produces malnourished children in the next generation. By offering counseling to expectant and nursing mothers and adolescent girls, the program tries to prevent malnutrition in the first place.
— Anthony Measham, task leader

Malnutrition is not always caused by poverty alone. It is often ignorance that leads to false caring practices. Educating women is just as important as supplementary feeding.
— G. Ramakrishnan, project coordinator

In the open air, nutrition and health workers (far left) learn how to identify high risk cases and help the mildly malnourished. The course encourages the workers to collaborate closely with one another, make frequent visits to the families they are helping, and maintain high ethical standards. The workers are reminded that false statistics, inflated results, and misuse of food will harm the women and children and undermine the project.

The health and nutrition workers pass on what they learn to women's and girl's groups (left). In turn, the groups are taught to transmit everything they learn to their neighbors.

HOW THE PROJECT WORKS

The Tamil Nadu Integrated Nutrition Project was the first World Bank project to make large-scale use of growth monitoring (of children 6–36 months old) as a means to target the most needy and monitor their progress. Growth monitoring is also an important educational tool to explain to mothers why one child is receiving food and another not and to give them objective feedback about how they are caring for their children.

Targeted supplementary feeding, the next essential project component, was an innovation that is now copied in many projects around the world. The feeding, for relatively brief periods, is focused on helping very young children recover their growth. Previous programs had concentrated on prolonged feeding of older children.

Above left: "We washermen have always been messengers. We pass information from village to village about births, deaths, and eligible matches." So Govindaswamy attended a project workshop for washermen, who traditionally wash all of the clothes used when a baby is delivered. Now he passes along information about nutrition.

Sivaraj, the priest (above right), gives the traditional amulet to protect the child malnourished and dehydrated by diarrhea—and a packet of oral rehydration salts. Sivaraj: "I have to start with the supernatural process so that the child's mother and grandmother may believe my words. But the real strength lies in these packets. I distribute 20 packets a month this way." The mother: "I myself have confidence in oral rehydration salts, but my mother-in-law insists that we call the priest when the baby is sick."

Muniyammal (right) a popular singer, uses song, dance, and drama to instill good dietary and health habits. "Give me the prose content, and I can convert it into a song," she says.

MASSIVE TRAINING OF HEALTH WORKERS AND
COMMUNITY PARTICIPATION

The program relies heavily on local nutrition workers, working in
conjunction with local women's and girls' groups. The groups are
taught behavior-change strategies. They learn to promote birth
weight recording, regular monthly weighing, and spot feeding. They
also participate in community assessment, analysis, and problem-
solving. They constantly proselytize to form new groups; thus, the
training is cascaded through the communities. To maintain vitality,
many women have formed credit and thrift societies, and have
taken on income-generating and micro-credit activities. Culturally
appropriate communication is incorporated into every aspect of
the project.

Teen tale-telling. *Once upon a time,
there was a king. He longed for an
heir, talented, bright, and beautiful.
"But, sire," said his minister, "the
child will have to be healthy. And the
best way to find out about health is
weight-for-age."*

63

Girls' and women's groups are taught how to promote the tenets of the project. In turn, they encourage others to form new groups and expand knowledge throughout their neighborhoods. Amateur street theater, right, plays an important role by reinforcing the messages for both the actors and the audience.

DATA COLLECTION ALLOWS CONTINUOUS MONITORING AND COURSE CORRECTIONS AS LESSONS ARE LEARNED

Field data go to Chennai (Madras) via modem, where they are collated. The analysis is relayed back to the districts for corrective action. For example, one report showed that the village of Salem had achieved a 79 percent early registration of pregnant women. In comparison, the accomplishment in Nagipattinam was a mere 39 percent. Door-to-door visits in Salem had made the difference. So the workers in Nagipattinam were instructed to make more visits, and the supervisors were told to be sure this was done.

Another weakness that showed up was that families were not changing the way they fed the children under two years of age. The project targeted more of its information and education to the parents of this youngest group, and later data collection showed substantial improvement in the children's diets and weight.

SUCCESS IN 20,000 VILLAGES

In 1994 the Bank's independent Operations Evaluation Department (OED) evaluated the first phase of the project. Noting that the project's nutrition interventions had been well implemented, OED provided many insights which have been incorporated into later phases of the project: Severe malnutrition had fallen significantly although moderate malnutrition was still quite widespread; and costs per beneficiary were lower than for less targeted nutrition programs.

Mothers who took part in the project knew much more about good nutrition and health practices than other mothers. They breastfed for longer, and fewer of their children needed supplementary feeding.

Over time, the project had increased its capacity to enroll the most needy—although coverage continued to be uneven from one place to another.

Some interventions were more useful than others: The frequency of weighing, younger age of enrollment, and immunization had a significant impact on nutritional status, while deworming and vitamin A supplements had not.

Malnutrition affects families unevenly. Once weighing and measuring has identified which children in the family are not growing normally, the program gives supplementary feeding only to those children and just until their growth is back on track. This feature makes the program cost effective. Healthy children (left) attending an "edutainment" event have a little snack.

Universal feeding was shown not to be necessary to achieve substantial nutritional and health gains.

The evaluators pointed to some of the reasons for the project's success: The project had taken great care in planning and execution. It had carefully selected and trained the community nutrition workers. The instructors themselves had been mobilized and trained at the level of small neighborhoods. Methodical and detailed work routines were set up. The project gave strong emphasis to supportive supervision and on-the-job training and made many successful efforts to gain community support. Finally, there was an emphasis on accurate monitoring and systematic use of the monitoring data for troubleshooting and feedback.

WHAT IS NEEDED NEXT

The national and state governments of India have mounted many large-scale nutrition programs. Dr. Anthony Measham and Dr. Meera Chatterjee report in *Wasting Away: The Crisis of Malnutrition in India* (World Bank, 1999) that unfortunately these programs have limited coverage and uneven quality. Although there is a good policy framework in place, the study concludes that India is wasting millions of dollars because the programs have major problems in targeting, implementation, and coverage. By virtue of almost 20 years' experience in addressing such problems, Tamil Nadu has increasingly refined its solutions and can offer a model for other programs. The World Bank is continuing its support for Tamil Nadu and is assisting four other Indian states to mount similar programs.

PROJECT TEAM

Peter Heywood, Anthony Measham, Richard Cambridge, James Greene, David Klaus, team leaders. Alan Berg, Selina Chaubey, Dr. Contractor, Dr. Govinidi, Richard Heaver, Renaldo Martorell, Chris Niesterowicz, Meera Priyadarshi, G. Ramakrishnan, Ellen Schaengold, Renata Seidel, R. Sethuraman, Nira Singh, Richard Skolnik, P. Subramanian. Edwin R. Lim, country director.

NOTE: This story draws information and photos from the monograph, *Catch them Young*, by Selina Chaubey, The World Bank, 1998.

Madagascar

FIGHTING MALNUTRITION ON THE RED ISLAND

Rare lizard (above), one of many species native to the "Red Island" of Madagascar, a country too poor to protect its biodiversity or feed its people.

Jao and his wife, Lala (left) are characters in a series of counseling cards used to teach maternal and child health, and nutrition. They have posted their "Arahabaina" diploma to show that their baby, Solofo, has been immunized against six diseases.

Brimming with unique plant and animal species, strange mountains, and impenetrable forests, Madagascar is a magnet for adventure travelers. That it is among of the least developed countries in the world is one of its charms, at least for tourists. For the vast majority of Malgaches, though, underdevelopment means lifelong poverty, illiteracy, and chronic malnutrition. Lack of knowledge, poor feeding practices, food scarcity, and sheer poverty all figure in the tragedy of hunger. Under such circumstances, it is pretty difficult for people to take care of the environment.

In this, one of the world's most impoverished countries, an alliance of Malgaches and donors has begun to show how malnutrition can be vanquished. SEECALINE (Surveillance et Éducation des Écoles et des Communautés en matière d'Alimentation et de Nutrition Élargie) is a highly successful Malgache response to the hardships of food insecurity and malnutrition. It is supported by the World Bank and six bilateral and multilateral assistance agencies.

THE BATTLE IS JOINED

PROJECT I, 1993–99. The Food Security and Nutrition Project was the first in Madagascar of its scope and size to work with communities and nongovernment organizations. The project focused on two

Rakoto is poor, his children don't have enough to eat. Rakoto is an endangered species but there is no SOS for him. Don't tell him your absurdities about protecting eagles, lemurs, and turtles. As long as Rakoto is starving, he'll eat them.

— *"Resa Babakoto," song by Rossy, Madagascar's most famous musician.*

Overview

FOOD SECURITY AND NUTRITION, 1993-1999

COMMUNITY AND SCHOOL NUTRITION, NUTRITION EDUCATION AND SURVEILLANCE, 1998-2003

The first project, focusing on two provinces with extreme food scarcities, trained mothers in proper weaning and nutrition practices, monitored and promoted the growth of almost half a million children, and gave food supplements where needed. The project also conducted a national campaign for iodized salt. (Iodine prevents goiter and cretinism.) The second project covers the entire country and targets almost a million children under three, 2.5 million up to 14 years, and more than 700,000 pregnant or lactating women. Most live in rural areas.

Total financing: US$74 million
Bank Group (International Development Agency) contribution: US$49 million
Principal external partners: World Food Program, Food and Agriculture Organization, World Health Organization, UNICEF, Japanese foreign assistance, US Agency for International Development

GOALS

PROJECT I: Teach mothers how to make better use of available food and change their feeding practices. Give food supplements temporarily, to get low-weight children back on track.

PROJECT II: Continue with Project I goals; reduce underweight and Vitamin A deficiency, anemia, and parasites; and improve community awareness and capacity to take action.

PROJECT II TARGETS*: Reduce underweight and vitamin A deficiency in children under 3 by 30 percent; reduce iron deficiency anemia among primary school children by 25 percent; and reduce helminth infections (parasites) among 3–14 year olds by 25 percent.

MADAGASCAR AT A GLANCE

Population: 14.6 million
Land area: 582,000 sq km
GNP: US$3.8 billion
GNP per capita: US$260
Poverty: Not available

Urban population: 28% of total population
Life expectancy at birth: 58 years
Infant mortality: 94 per 1,000 live births

Child malnutrition: 34% (of children under 5)
Access to safe water: 16% (of total population)
Illiteracy: 46% (of population age 15 and older)

* See Appendix 1 for monitoring and evaluation information.

It starts with the children. Half the children under five are stunted from chronic malnutrition. Ten-year-olds often look like they are six. This girl (left) is as proud and excited as if she were being photographed in a white pinafore. She takes care of her brother and their begging bowl in Fianarantsoa, a southern provincial capital; but she usually forgets to ask for anything. She is not part of some cynical begging industry. She's just helping her hungry family.

provinces suffering from extreme food scarcities, Antananarivo and Toliary. The project trained mothers, monitored and promoted the growth of almost half a million children, and gave food supplements where needed. The project also conducted a national campaign for iodized salt. (Iodine prevents goiter and cretinism.)

PROJECT II, 1998–2003. Although Project I was highly successful in the targeted provinces, only the iodized salt campaign had national impact. If anything, due to economic stagnation, hunger in Madagascar was worse in 1997 than in 1993. Thus, an expanded program was sorely needed. The second project, which covers the entire country, targets almost a million children under three, 2.5 million up to 14 years, and more than 700,000 pregnant or lactating women. Most live in rural areas.

The scope also has dramatically increased: Reduce underweight and vitamin A deficiency in children under three by 30 percent; reduce iron deficiency anemia among primary school children by 25 percent; reduce helminth infections (parasites) among 3- to 14-year-olds by 25 percent; and improve community awareness and capacity to take action.

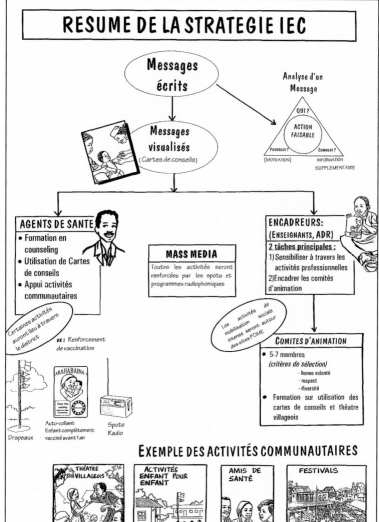

"The Information, Education and Communication Strategy" of SEECALINE.

First, the health professionals identify the messages to be delivered, considering how many can realistically be gotten across and which are the most important. Doable actions are key. The professionals build the strategy around an analysis of who should take the action, how the action should be carried out, and what motivation should be appealed to.

Written messages are developed and translated into counseling cards, radio spots, and programming.

At the local level, community nutrition workers and training coordinators (these may be drawn from teachers or government workers who know how to read) learn how to use the counseling cards and facilitate community activities. "Comites d'Animation," comprising diverse villagers who are respected and liked, also learn to use the counseling cards and put on village theater, children's entertainment, and festivals.

This brother and sister live in the middle of nowhere, in Zomandao, a dusty settlement of 800 people, mostly cattle herders. Depending on weather, the rutted dirt road leading three hours from the small town of Ambavalao to Zomandao is barely more than a track, passable by jeep. In 1996, the government had plans to upgrade Zomandao's health clinic, a wooden shelter open to the breezes, devoid of furniture or equipment.

A starchy, immaculate midwife named Lilie visits from Ambavalao when her motorbike is in repair and has gas. Or she catches a ride with someone. The only vehicle in Zomandao is a bicycle.

Providing health and nutrition information in Zomandao is a challenge. There are no newspapers, and in any case, many of the people are illiterate. There is no television and no electricity. A wind-up radio and loud speakers—unhoped-for luxuries—could broadcast mass media messages for children and mothers. Until such amenities arrive, the midwife, a local health committee, village festivities, flags for immunization days, and counseling cards (see following pages) can accomplish much.

Health agents, community nutrition workers, teachers, nurses, and midwives all over Madagascar tell the stories that are printed on the back of the laminated counseling cards and thus can deliver many sound messages about health.

Right: Fathers are important, too. Solofo is getting bigger. Jao wants to be sure the baby gets enough food. Every day, he brings snacks from the market. The counseling card says that, in addition to three square meals, the child should get two healthy snacks, especially fruits with yellow-orange flesh. Jao also takes good care of his nursing wife. He tells her to eat well and drink enough liquids. He makes her rice with fruit to help her produce good quality milk.

Bottom right: Solofo has blood in his feces. He won't drink. He is lethargic and vomits. For three days, he has had diarrhea and a fever. The worried parents decide to take him to the health clinic, where Fanja, the medic, assures them that they have done the right thing. He tells them what to do, and after several days, the baby is better.

Opposite: Lala explains, "A baby under six months has to feed 10 times a day, including at night. That is what I do, and that is why I have enough milk." The message adds that breastfeeding at night helps the family to space its babies by reducing fertility. (The counseling cards are the conception of the Academy for Educational Development, Washington, D.C., and the USAID-funded BASICS project.)

Life expectancy in Madagascar is actually declining. The first project showed how we could begin to reverse this desperate situation:

There was a highly significant impact on children newborn to three. In the target communities with nutrition sites, the rate of malnutrition among these children decreased by about 58 percent in Antananarivo Province and 48 percent in the Toliary Province target areas.

The national iodized salt campaign made a tremendous difference. The goiter prevalence in pregnant women and school children decreased from 45 percent in 1992 to 15 percent in 1998!

SEECALINE has really reached people. Many baby girls are now named 'Secaline.' I think this recognition can be attributed to the success of the program.

— Michelle Ratsivalaka, SEECALINE's national director

Ten international agencies, a university, and six ministries have agreed with SEECALINE to deliver the same communications through their various programs across Madagascar. The ministries usually have local employees, such as agricultural extension agents or postal workers, who can help communities to play their part.

Teacher and students illustrated on the counseling card (right) get into the act. The back of the card provides the story, to be read to community members: a boy named Niry is proudly raising three flags. The teacher explains, "The three flags indicate that in three days, there will be a vaccination day. When you get home, tell your family."

The counseling card provides further information: "Teachers, health agents, and local authorities! Put the flags up: yellow, blue and green—three days in advance; yellow and blue— two days before; and yellow alone the night before vaccination day. By taking responsibility, we will help protect our children. Parents, check your child's vaccination card to be sure you haven't forgotten."

There are many groups and projects working on maternal and child health and nutrition in Madagascar. In 1998, these groups came together to harmonize nutrition messages, and a communications task force was created. The groups continue to work together to identify, discuss, and promote the same messages to their common audiences.

Deciding on messages is a major challenge. Which are the most effective and essential behaviors? How many messages can be gotten across? The key is to identify simple, doable behaviors that will make the biggest difference. The messages cover infant growth monitoring, mother care, breast-feeding, complementary feeding (of a fortified food mix, to mothers-to-be and malnourished children), micro-nutrients (Vitamin A, iodine, and iron), food hygiene, and the prevention of sexually transmitted diseases. All have been market-tested.

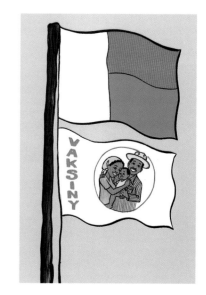

INFORMATION, EDUCATION, AND COMMUNICATION TASK FORCE

Ministries of Health, Agriculture, Secondary and Primary Education, Finance and Economy, Commerce and Consumption, and Scientific Research; University of Antananarivo, UNICEF, World Health Organization, World Food Program, SEECALINE, Food and Agriculture Organization, U.S. Agency for International Development, Catholic Relief Services, CARE International, Peace Corps, and the Seventh Day Adventist Health Program.

PROJECT TEAM

Richard Seifman, Marie-Odile Waty, and Eileen Murray, task managers. Michelle Ratsivalaka, national project director. Bertrand Ah-Sue, Michel Andrien, Alan Berg, Donald Bundy, Madeleine Epote, David Freese, Paul Geli, Jacques Gruloos, T. Mpoy-Kamulayi, Michele Lioy, Martine Lugat, Judith McGuire, Sigal Nissan-Felber, Gervais Rakotoarimanana, Sylvain Rambeloson, Christian Rey, Claudia Rokx, Raj Soopramanien. Michael Sarris, country director. Philippe Le Houerou, resident representative.

Nutrition programs around the world have shown that even the very poor can improve their nutrition. The secret lies in proper breast-feeding and weaning and in knowing which local, low-cost foods are nutritious. Sound nutrition must begin before birth, with the mother, and continue through life. Thus, communication and counseling are vital, and we have made them central to the program in Madagascar.

—Richard Seifman, task manager

Uganda

A HEALTHY START FOR UGANDA'S CHILDREN

A colorful chart (above) dramatizes the most important information for caretakers and children: height and weight. If these are on track, the child is getting enough nutritious food. Left: preschool, Uganda style, with songs, drums, and smiles.

More than 12 percent of Uganda's children die before their first birthday. Many who survive suffer from malnutrition and disease and do poorly in school. Malnutrition is high for a fertile country with a relatively stable food supply. About one in four preschool children are underweight for their age, and two in five are stunted.

Poor feeding practices, a high incidence of infectious diseases, a low level of education among mothers, and poverty are all factors. Both children and their mothers lack iron, iodine, Vitamin A, and other micronutrients in their diets. The consequences are low birth weight, goiter, reduced mental capacity, and even cretinism.

The aftermath of the Ugandan civil war and the AIDS epidemic compound these problems. More than a million orphans are thrown onto their communities for care.

*Banana fronds and
smoke-plumed villages fill
a landscape of wild sunlit
colors set against purple
clouds. Graceful people in
white shirts and bright
kangas walk everywhere
along red roads ... , and
the umbrella, jitney bus,
and bicycle are ubiquitous
... in [this] country of
heavy humid leaves and
bruised thick skies....*

— Peter Mattheissen,
The Tree Where Man was Born

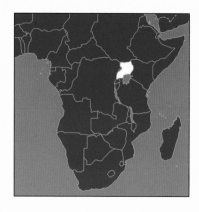

Overview

NUTRITION AND EARLY CHILDHOOD DEVELOPMENT PROJECT,
1998-2003

Covering 8,000 communities in 25 of Uganda's 45 districts, the project teaches better feeding and child care practices. Working through local nonprofit organizations, the project also makes grants for community micro-projects that promote the well being of children.

Total cost: US$40 million; World Bank (International Development Agency) US$34 million
Partners: WHO, UNICEF, SmithKline Beecham, nonprofit organizations

GOALS *

Halve malnutrition among preschool children in the target areas by 2003.

Increase their readiness for school.

Reduce the costs of having children drop out and repeat grades due to malnutrition and diminished ability to perform.

Increase families' opportunities to earn income.

UGANDA AT A GLANCE

Population: 20.9 million

Land area: 200,000 sq km

GNP: US$6.7 billion

GNP per capita: US$320

Poverty: 46%
(percent of population below
national poverty line)

Urban population: 13% of
total population

Life expectancy at birth:
42 years

Infant mortality: 99 per 1,000
live births

Child malnutrition: 26%
(of children under 5)

Access to safe water: 41%
(of total population)

Illiteracy: 42%
(of population age 15 and
older)

* See Appendix 1 for monitoring and evaluation information.

I didn't know my child was malnourished. All of the children in the village look like this. — A mother

Uganda is a fertile country. Just toss a seed and it will grow. So what we have is a big job of advocacy, training, and communication. In fact, I think perhaps the most unusual feature of this project is that we do not have much in the way of physical inputs other than weighing scales, preschool materials, seeds, and gardening tools. The real outputs are community skills in child rearing and diet, gardening, and improved incomes which enable people to purchase additional food.
— Marito Garcia, task manager

Children caring for children (left). There are more than a million orphans of AIDS and civil war.

Malnutrition has many facets.
The pool in which the boy is standing
(left) probably contains worms that
can enter the boy's feet and stay in his
belly. The worms suck a liter and a
half of blood every year and result in
anemia and learning problems.

Of the three boys playing (above) the
one on the right has worms. No
matter how much he eats, the worms
get part of it. Plantain banana trees
(in the background) grow everywhere.
Mothers mash the fruit and give it as
weaning food to their babies. This
food, called Matooke, is filling, but it
has almost no nutritional value.

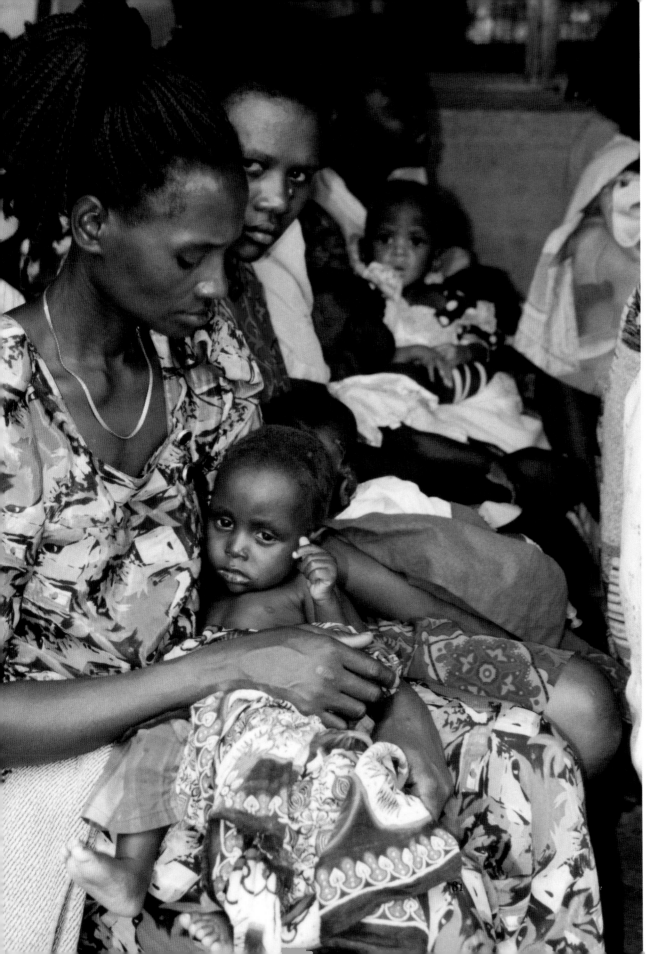

Parents can learn to prevent and seek care for worm infestations. They can learn to feed their children nutritious, inexpensive, and locally grown foods. The Nutrition and Child Development Project is set up to deliver such information and to foster healthier practices. Like many nutrition projects, this one gives high priority to growth monitoring. When the mothers bring their children in for weighing and measuring, the children also get immunizations. Mothers also receive pre- and postnatal care and counseling. The project relies on nonprofit organizations to mobilize parents and surrogate parents.

The Nutrition and Child Development Project covers 8,000 communities in 25 of Uganda's 45 districts. Its approach is to teach better child care practices, including those that will improve psycho-social and cognitive development and increase families' opportunities to earn income.

The project expects to halve malnutrition among preschool children in the target areas by 2003, thereby increasing their readiness for school and supporting Uganda's drive for universal primary education. An underlying principle is that early childhood development will ultimately pay for itself by reducing the costs of having children drop out and repeat grades.

WEIGHING AND MEASURING, DEMONSTRATIONS AND COUNSELING, PRESCHOOLS, HEALTH CENTERS, KITCHEN GARDENS

The project's approach is to help develop pre-schools and health centers and to teach alternatives to traditional behaviors. Other components include growth monitoring, immunizations, pre- and postnatal care and counseling, and cooking and gardening demonstrations. Nongovernment organizations mobilize the parents and surrogate parents and provide facilitation at the community level.

CREATING AWARENESS, CHANGING BEHAVIOR

Child fairs are a major feature of the project. Twelve villages are invited to each fair. There are competitions, counseling, weighing of children, immunizations, and cooking demonstrations. The educational messages promoted through the child fairs are reinforced by radio talk shows and street theater.

SUPPORTING COMMUNITY PROJECTS

The project makes grants for community micro-projects that promote the well-being of children. Local nonprofit organizations help the communities assess needs, propose activities, and apply for the grants. The grants pay for such items as daycare materials, gardening tools, and seeds. The nonprofit organizations provide

---

CHILD HEALTH CARD

REPUBLIC OF UGANDA — MINISTRY OF HEALTH

Health Unit		Child's No.	
Child's Name			
Sex	Date of birth	Birth Order	
Mother's Name		Mother's Occupation	
Father's Name		Father's Occupation	
Where the Family lives			

IMMUNISATIONS AND VITAMIN A

	0	1	2	3
		write in date of immunisation		
BCG				
POLIO				
DPT				
MEASLES				
VITAMIN A				

IMMUNISE TO PROTECT YOUR CHILD; HAVE ALL IMMUNISATIONS DONE BEFORE THE FIRST BIRTH DAY

Getting the messages out is a challenge in a country where rural people may have little ability to read and no access to newspapers or television. Although radio supposedly covers about 70 percent of the population, many Ugandans don't have electricity and can't afford batteries for their radios. Even where mass media does reach people, lasting behavior change can take a lot of personal persuasion and teaching. These are the reasons the project relies heavily on village-level counselors with health cards, training, demonstrations, and child fairs.

At SmithKline Beecham, we use communications techniques to market commercial products and services. SmithKline has lent me to the project for a year because we are convinced that communication can be used equally well to promote behaviors that will improve health and well-being.

The communications messages cover deworming, personal hygiene, the importance of clean water and sanitation; and feeding and weaning practices to diminish stunting. These messages also discuss what to plant in kitchen gardens; substitutes and supplements for Matooke (plantain). In addition, fathers are encouraged to play with their children, a valuable contribution to growth and one that is not the custom in Uganda.

—Caroline Pond of SmithKline Beecham, an international company that is supporting the communications activities of the project

technical supervision and training in such skills as savings, management, and basic accounting. For their part, communities contribute goods or services. A major feature of the project is children's psychological and social development, with an effort to promote preschools and to encourage fathers and mothers to play with their children.

PROJECT TEAM

Marito Garcia, task manager. Preeti Ahuja, Harold Alderman, Donald Bundy, Claudine Cobra, Mary Eming Young, Patrice Engle, Gita Gopal, Mary Green, Andrew Hall, Randolph Harris, Ruth Kagia, Joseph Kizito, Jennifer Lawrence, Mbuba Mbungu, Harriet Nannyonjo, Christine Pena, Caroline Pond, Vanessa Saldanha, E. V. Shantha, William Steel, Caby Verzosa, Palitha Wijesinghe, Fred Wood, Aberra Zerabruk. James W. Adams-country director.

Peru

PEACE, FARMING, AND FORESTRY

Six years ago, guerrillas fighters might have murdered an outsider. Now, in the high Sierras, World Bank staff are helping the Quechua Indians rebuild pre-Hispanic terraces and irrigation systems, replant decimated forests, and start women's businesses. Modern farming and conservation, combined with ancient tools and practices, are giving hope to this beautiful region. The Bank Group's country assistance strategy for Peru concentrates on poverty reduction. The Sierra Natural Resources Management and Poverty Alleviation Project (PRONAMACHCS) helps seven very poor departments of the Peruvian Sierras by tapping an award-winning formula of the Ministry of Agriculture and the U.S. Agency for International Development. The project aims at communities that previously were centers of civil unrest and supports investments in micro-projects to raise incomes and conserve natural resources. Villagers play a big role in choice, design, and execution. By donating their labor, they contribute around 30 percent of the micro-project costs.

TARGETING AND GOALS

The geographic unit for planning and implementing the project is the watershed basin. The project covers 125 such micro-basins, which are home to 75,000 people living in in extreme poverty.

Carmencita (above) helps her mom prepare potatoes for market in a village that has no school, doctor, or nurse. In the village of Churcampa (opposite), the women take turns with the beekeeping, so that they can keep up with their farm duties and also gain extra income. Potato processing and beekeeping are among new women's enterprises in Peru's high Sierras.

85

Overview

SIERRA NATURAL RESOURCES MANAGEMENT AND POVERTY
ALLEVIATION PROJECT (PRONAMACHCS), 1996-2002

The project helps seven very poor departments of the Peruvian Sierras with micro-projects to raise incomes and conserve natural resources. The project covers approximately 75,000 people.

Total financing: US$93 million

Bank Group contribution: US$51 million (International Bank for Reconstruction and Development)

GOALS

Support investments in micro-projects.

Raise incomes and conserve natural resources.

Involve villagers in the choice, design, and execution of the projects.

2001 TARGETS IN THE PROJECT AREAS[1]

Benefit 75,000 families.

Increase farming production by 25 percent.

Increase cultivation in rehabilitated areas by 90 percent.

Increase the areas under agroforestry protection by 25 percent.

Increase the number of producers using improved seeds by 25 percent.

Bring 20 percent of the women into project participation.

PERU AT A GLANCE

Population: 24.8 million

Land area: 1,280,000 sq km

GNP: US$61.1 billion

GNP per capita: US$2,460

Poverty: 49% (of population below national poverty line)

Urban population: 72% of total population

Life expectancy at birth: 69 years

Infant mortality: 40 per 1,000 live births

Child malnutrition: 8% (of children under 5)

Access to safe water: 66% (of total population)

Illiteracy: 11% (of population age 15 and older)

* See Appendix 1 for monitoring and evaluation information.

Succeeding with community participation is not easy. It means overcoming centuries of deference and dependence upon the patron—whether Inca, Spaniard, or big landowner.

— Steve Oliver, senior agricultural economist (below)

TRANQUIL LAND, BRUTAL HISTORY

The Incas ruled. Then came the Spanish conquistadors. They transformed the ancient Inca holdings into large farms. Many Quechua villagers became landless laborers and remained so until the 1969 Agrarian Reform.

The aristocrats came and went. But the Quechua were always there, laboring for the patron. Then, in the 1980s, came the Shining Path. Often shooting at anyone resisting, the Shining Path terrorists would come into the villages to loot and recruit young members. Then the Army would come and punish the villagers for providing food and soldiers to the guerrillas. Many villagers fled for the city.

"Finally," says Steve Oliver, economist, "the government and USAID came in with a different message: 'Let's talk about hope and alternatives. You have a tradition of communal work. What projects do you need and want? What can you, the communities, put in?' And that was the beginning of what has become the PRONAMACHCS project."

With support from PRONAMACHCS, community workers help design the community development plan, presenting a "recipe book" of possibilities (above), and the people form committees and choose what they want to do.

They draw up an agreement that lays out the responsibilities of both the community and the executing agency (a nongovernmental organization or local government office).

The project teaches the people how to set up a business and plow earnings back to make it grow, how to set up a bank account, and how to do the work. Seed money from the executing agency, for tools or small equipment, is matched by contributions of community labor.

The community is invited to start with basic works, such as terracing, soil erosion control, or reforestation. Over time, the villagers prove themselves and gain confidence. Notice the picks (opposite). These tools go far back in Quechua tradition.

The rebuilding of terraces represents a return to ancient soil conservation practices. This is a very important element of the project. Revitalized irrigation and improved farming practices, such as contour farming, are also having a positive environmental impact.

The project moves step by step, as fast as the people want. With technical assistance the villagers can move to a more demanding project, such as a complete, if small, irrigation system. Irrigation reservoir (above right).

In the third year, if the people want to do so, the project works with them to set up a rotating fund. The community committees can borrow to buy inputs, such as seeds and fertilizer. But now they must repay the money.

I believe that Bank projects will be successful only if the people who will benefit are involved in the design and execution.

I had the assignment of figuring out how we could best accomplish this in the Sierra project—by studying the social mores and institutions. Through the study, it became clear that the Incas and the Quechua both gave—and their descendents continue to give—higher priority to the family and to common good than to the individual.

They also attach very high value to the principles of 'don't steal and don't lie.' The participatory approach builds upon these traditions, and I think this underlies the success of the project.
— Maria Elena Castro, social scientist

ESTABLISHING SELF-SUFFICIENCY

The women have made a business of their traditional cactus sugar. In the past, they could not sell to a large market because they didn't have a uniform product in sufficient quantities. Now they have formed a working group. They rent extra land, work in turns, and maintain a little warehouse from which they sell their products. With the project's contribution, they have bought a scale, cups, bags, tools, and filtering equipment. PRONAMACHCS staff has trained them in management, marketing, and quality control. Thus the women have standardized their product; and they produce in volume so that they can sell it to traders, who in turn haul the bags off to market in town.

THE ENVIRONMENTAL ANGLE

These beautiful lands have lost 60 percent of their forest cover. Slash-and-burn agriculture, abandonment of more than 1 million hectares of Inca terraces, and overgrazing have all done their damage.

The project seeks to bring one-quarter of the land in the watershed basins under integrated agroforestry management. To accomplish this, the project is helping the farmers to establish resource management committees and training them to control pests, protect trees against damage by domestic animals, manage regrowth, and integrate environmentally sound practices into both their farming and their forestry activities. In addition, the aim is to develop 540 communal tree nurseries, produce 20 million seedlings, and plant 17 million trees. The campesino nursery operators are able to sell their seedlings to forestry projects. Because this is a profit-making business, many communities are moving ahead on their own and copying one another even without project support.

PROJECT TEAM

Pierre Werbrouck, task manager. Musa Asad, Maria Elena Castro, Elizabeth Dasso, J. Escurra, Ivo Marzall, S. Raswant, Steven Oliver, Gladys Sakata. Isabel Guerrero, country director.

The men say the women have always tended to the farm animals and have done most of the work on the family plot, and this should not change. At left, the women cut the cactus, boil down the liquid, let it solidify, and package it. They have scheduled their work so as not to interfere with their customary duties.

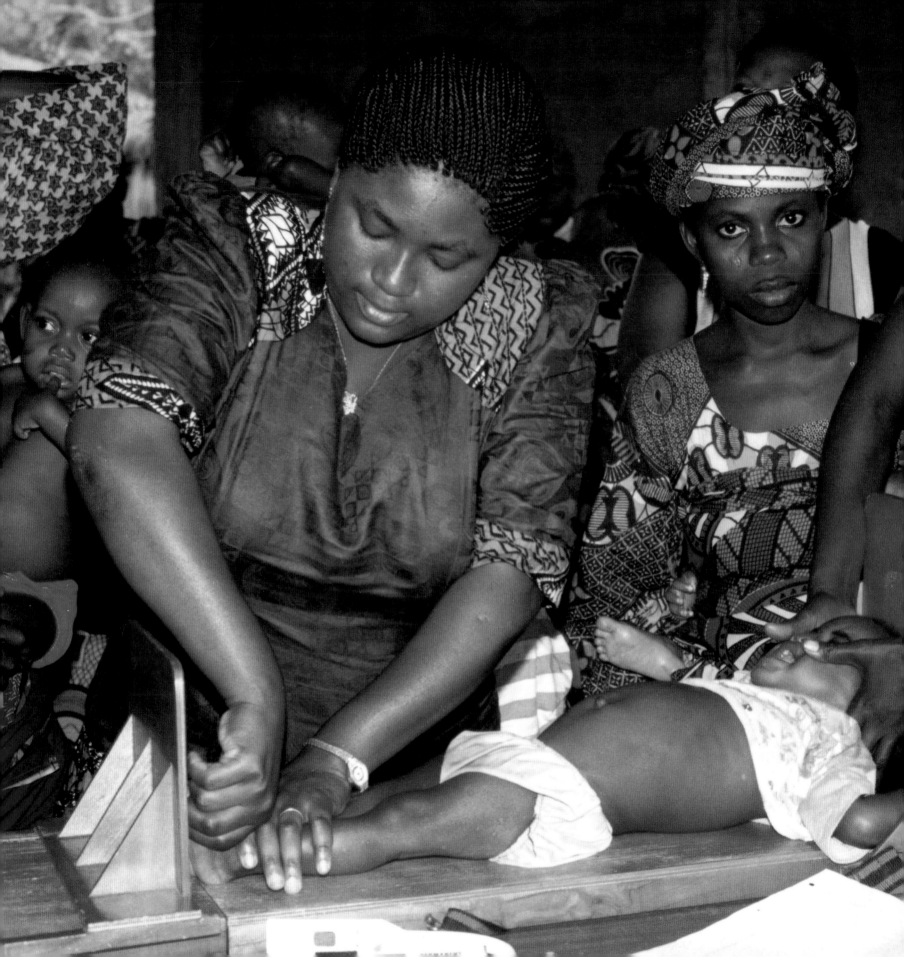

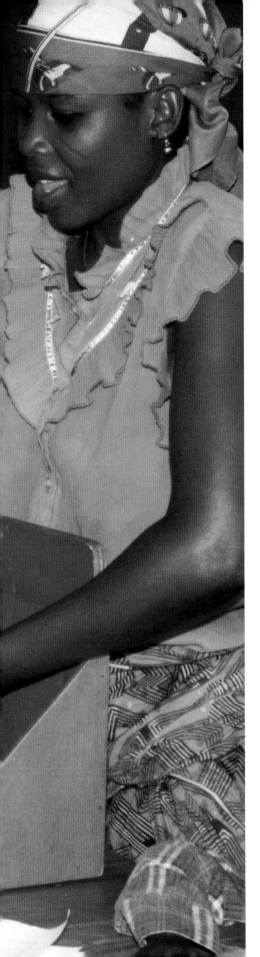

Benin

FOOD WHERE THERE WAS NONE

One in three children is malnourished. The Community-based Food Security Project aims to change this, by teaching parents to recognize and reverse malnutrition. Tracking the height and weight of the children is the test. More and better food is the solution.

Benin is generally self-sufficient in food, but one in five adults and one in three children goes to bed hungry every night. In some pockets of the country, food scarcity is chronic. In others, it fluctuates from year to year. Areas where food supplies are scarce or unreliable dot the south where landholdings are small and degraded; northern areas of poor soil and erosion; and some parts of the coast where fisheries are depleted. Most of these locales are very remote. They receive no public services nor much of anything else. Virtually to a person, the citizens in these areas are the poorest of the poor.

In the past, the government did not know how to tackle the issue of food security. The attempts to control the food market through storage, processing, and market interventions have had little effect this far off the beaten path. In fact, because no one knows what to do, the subject was officially taboo. Now, with the support of the Community-based Food Security Project (PILSA), the Ministry of Agriculture is providing micro-credits for simple agricultural, fishery, and commercial investments that the villagers choose and to which they contribute. These activities provide jobs and regular access to food.

The project also aims to reduce malnutrition rates, especially among children under five years old and pregnant and lactating

93

Overview

COMMUNITY-BASED FOOD SECURITY PROJECT (PILSA), 1995-2000

PILSA supports the Ministry of Agriculture's micro-credits to villages for simple agricultural, fishery and commercial investments that the villagers choose and contribute to. Non-governmental organizations (NGOs) provide the link between the ministry and the villages.

Total cost: US$19 million; World Bank (International Development Agency): US$10 million

External partners: Danish Aid (DANIDA), Benin National University, World Food Program

GOALS

Provide jobs and regular access to food.

Reduce malnutrition rates, especially among children under five years old and pregnant and lactating women.

IMPACT IN THE PROJECT AREA BY THE END OF 1997 *

Introduced 1,160 micro-projects.
Benefited almost 32,000 people directly and 70,000 indirectly.
Brought almost 18,000 children under growth and health surveillance.
Brought 800 pregnant women and 4,500 lactating women under supervision.
Reduced malnutrition by 17 percent.

BENIN AT A GLANCE

Population: 6 million

Land area: 111,000 sq km

GNP : US$2.3 billion

GNP per capita: US$380

Poverty: 33% (of population below national poverty line)

Urban population: 41% of total population

Life expectancy at birth: 53 years

Infant mortality: 88 per 1,000 live births

Child malnutrition: 29% (of children under 5)

Access to safe water: 72% (of total population)

Illiteracy: 66% (of population age 15 and older)

* *See Appendix 1 for monitoring and evaluation information.*

women. In total, project activities are expected to benefit 100,000 rural people directly. Infrastructure works are expected to benefit about 300,000 people.

HOW IT WORKS

The project contracts with nongovernmental organizations, which hire and manage community workers. The workers, in turn, help the villagers select and organize micro-projects. All of the micro-projects are supposed to have something to do with food security.

The villagers decide what work or money they will offer as their part of the bargain. The sponsoring organization writes a proposal to conform to the project's operations manual. The villagers and their chief review the proposal.

Local officials then conduct a second review to see if the proposals are feasible, determine whether they fit with government plans, and evaluate the need for funds. How many groups are asking for similar projects? What are the experiences, commitments and reputations of the villagers proposing the projects? What kinds of technical assistance and training will the groups need, and who will provide these? When such practical questions are answered satisfactorily, the loan is made and the micro-project begins. Every aspect of the project supports the villagers.

SUBSIDIZED NUTRITION AND HEALTH WORKERS—FOR NOW

In addition to the micro-projects, by the end of 1998, the project had 20,000 children and 5,000 pregnant and/or lactating women under supervision. The villagers select a community nutrition worker who is trained by the nongovernmental organizations and given a bicycle and medical supplies. In close cooperation with the local health district, the worker seeks to identify malnutrition at an early stage, teaches the parents what to do, and contacts the nearest health post when needed.

The PILSA approach has been so successful that the goal of 400 micro-projects was met halfway through implementation. So the project shifted funds from other components and had 1600 micro-projects under way by 1999. The woman below is going to the market to sell cassava.

With micro-loans from the PILSA project, the villagers have chosen to buy more farmland, construct small irrigation systems, build cereal banks, set up food processing operations, expand market crops, open nurseries and fisheries, and start small trading and marketing businesses. Men plowing (right) will grow mangoes, coconuts, and papayas to be sold locally. Women (below) adroitly care for their children while processing coconut oil to sell.

Transparency is our watchword. We are very strict with everyone in this project. Everyone has to comply with the project manual. I am not popular with everyone, but the way we can make the project and this country succeed is by following the rules.
— Benjamin Soude, project manager

In the seedling cooperative (left), the seedlings will be used for reforestation.

Most projects bring both triumphs and problems, and PILSA has been no different.

The performance of the nongovernmental organizations hired to work with the communities was uneven, to say the least. Some organizations were charging 1,000 percent overhead; others were overbilling for field staff salaries or falsifying the amounts being transferred to the communities. The entities were not all local. Some of them were large, international organizations. At this point, the Bank's supervision team required the project to take corrective action. Fortunately, the local project director had the authority and integrity to take drastic measures, although at considerable personal and political risk. After a thorough review of the portfolio, he permanently removed six of the 28 organizations working on the project. The Bank team concluded the best way to avoid such malfeasance in the future would be to reselect the nongovernmental groups annually and eliminate the bottom third of the performers.

Benjamin Soude, the local project manager (left) has directed four World Bank projects. Other Benin Food Security Project team members, continuing from left to right: Madani M. Tall, task manager; Thierry Brun, Ousa Sananikone; and Mogens Pederson of Danida, the Danish aid agency.

To encourage the villagers to value the health and nutrition services provided by the community worker and influence them to follow the counseling they are given, the PILSA project requires villagers to pay at least nominal fees.

As for the NGOs, we compensate them on a different basis now. Because they used to earn 10 percent on the investment value of the microprojects, they leaned toward big projects. To encourage smaller projects, we have now put a ceiling on the NGOs' share.

— Madani M. Tall, task manager

The project adopted this approach and turned around as a result.

"We are getting smarter," says Madani Tall, task manager. "In another project, women were paid to bring their children to be weighed. They took the money—but didn't give the children more food. So the PILSA project encourages the families to pay nominal fees for the health and nutrition services. We hope that the villagers will soon be making enough money on their projects to pay higher fees to the health workers, or at least cover their transport; and to pay the villager worker, as well, if they think he or she is doing a good job.

"As for the NGOs, we've revised their incentives. At the beginning, the project bought cars and motorcycles for some. This was nonsense. Now we say, 'buy your own car or motorcycle. The project will pay for the gas.'"

BURGEONING DEMAND AND IMPACT

Halfway through implementation, PILSA had met its objective of funding 400 village micro-projects, many of them profitable ventures. When people saw their neighbors making money, they requested their own projects. By mid-1998, the project was supporting more than 1,600 micro-projects.

Not all of the 1,600 have revenue potential, and some are not going to survive over the long run. So, in 1999—the last year of this credit—the project consolidated and shifted resources to the best micro-projects, in order to provide additional training and counseling and nurture them to the point where they could become truly effective. The project has had a dramatic impact on malnutrition in the target areas: 30 percent reduction in four years. Said one villager, "We used to dig a lot of tiny graves. Now we don't have to. We aren't burying children any more."

PROJECT TEAM

Nicolas Ahouissoussi, Madani M. Tall, task managers. Michel Aklamavo, Adolpho Brizzi, Thierry Brun, Abdou Salam Drabo, Soulemane Fofana, Wilda Sajous, Ousa Sananikone, Benjamin Soude. Theodore Ahlers, country director.

As the micro-projects progress, the villagers are taught management, simple accounting, and how to price their services (top). They are encouraged to establish local banking relationships and shown how to demonstrate their creditworthiness. At the end of three years, the successful projects will have repaid their original PILSA loans.

They are then expected to "graduate" and, henceforth, to borrow directly from the local savings and loan association.

These women (above) are learning about breast-feeding, the oldest and most sanitary form of food security for infants.

Mali

Desert home of ancient empires, crossed with the ghosts of old caravans, Mali conjures up visions of the fabled library and scholarship of Timbuktu, and the riches of precolonial trade. Mali today is a treasure trove of old Islamic manuscripts and artifacts and home to a diverse and fascinating culture. Mali is also one of the world's poorest countries. Hunger is no stranger to its growing population.

THE PROJECT

The Grass-Roots Initiative to Fight Hunger and Poverty Project is helping to reduce poverty in the most vulnerable rural communities in Mali. Its approach is to help people help themselves by relying on government and civil society to collaborate in the development effort. The project responds to community priorities for basic training. Using a learning-by-doing approach, the project involves communities from initial planning through monitoring and evaluation. The project relies heavily on community organizations, nongovernmental organizations, and local authorities and, in the process, strengthens their relationships with one another.

"Sous l'arbre a palabre"—under the traditional palaver tree, the villagers of Mopti region, opposite, decide what small project they should undertake with a Bank-sponsored grant. A low-tech well, above.

101

You can't sweep with only one piece of straw, but by putting all the straws together, you can sweep the whole courtyard.

—Malian village saying

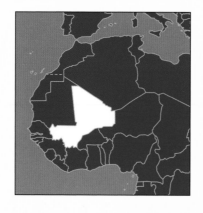

Overview

This project is helping to reduce poverty in the most vulnerable rural communities in Mali by helping people help themselves.

Total cost: US$23 million

World Bank (International Development Agency): US$21.5 million

GOALS *

Respond to community priorities for basic infrastructure and local capacity building. Sub-projects chosen by the communities include schools, small dams and irrigation projects, sanitation, and others.

Involve communities from initial planning through construction, management, and evaluation.

Work with community organizations, nongovernmental organizations (NGOs), and local authorities and strengthen their relationships with one another.

MALI AT A GLANCE

Population: 10.6 million

Land area: 1,220,000 sq km

GNP: US$2.6 billion

GNP per capita: US$250

Poverty: 63%
(percent of population below national poverty line)

Urban population:
29% of total population

Life expectancy at birth: 50 years

Infant mortality:
118 per 1,000 live births

Child malnutrition: 40%
(of children under 5)

Access to safe water:
48% of population

Illiteracy: 65%
(of population age 15 and older)

* See Appendix 1 for monitoring and evaluation information.

I am from Timbuktu, and I can tell you. We are right at the heart of the World.
— Ali Farka Toure, one of Mali's most famous musicians.

After the 17th century, when merchant shipping replaced ancient caravan routes, Mali was forgotten; but its rich cultural life remained and survives today. The name Timbuktu has the mysterious ring of unbridgeable distances, unless you happen to live there.

The project also has a component to strengthen local and national decision making on poverty issues, partly by establishing a permanent poverty monitoring system.

TARGETING

To select micro-project locations, the planners started with the poorest region, Mopti. They used survey and census data to rank regions, subregions, and villages by their income and spending levels; their need for schools, health centers, roads, wells, and credit facilities; and the nutritional status of their inhabitants. From among the most disadvantaged villages, the planners chose locations with around 500 inhabitants that were near other communities (to create synergies). Willingness to participate was the final decisive factor.

As a statistician, I am happy to see that the household surveys and population census that the Bank has supported over the years have produced data, which now have been used to target the project's resources. The use of the data gives a scientific basis to the targeting exercise and thus greater confidence that the project will benefit the poorest.

— Antoine Simonpietri, World Bank statistician

DISCUSSING, DECIDING AND FORMALLY AGREEING. *Strengthening decision making at the village level is a critical feature of the project. Through discussions of problems and solutions, villagers decide on their priorities and request financing. Village management committees are formed to make decisions during project activities. These committees enter into a contract for the investment in their village.*

LEARNING. *The village committees, which manage the sub-projects, attend literacy classes and are trained in management and in maintaining whatever micro-project is built. Village animateurs are trained in communication skills. A local nongovernmental organization facilitates the activities and the training and itself receives training in such subjects as participatory methods, communication skills, monitoring, and evaluation.*

It ain't easy. In one village meeting, the men said, "our women want a school above all," and the men supported this aspiration. I asked why there were no women on the committee. The men laughed sheepishly. Who knows? A little girl who goes to the school might be on the next committee.

— Adriana de Leva, task manager

DOING. *Sub-projects include schools, small dams, irrigation, and sanitation. Responsibilities are shared among the stakeholders. The manual of procedure, the "Bible" for project implementation, lays out the roles and responsibilities of each actor and the procurement and disbursement procedures. By requiring competitive bidding along Bank lines, the rules strongly encourage honesty and fair play.*

We have come a long way. In other countries, the government and NGOs may have a practice of working together. In Mali, three or four years ago, the NGOs never would have been called in, and that is what has made this project incredibly innovative. Now, they see each other as partners.
— Grace Yabrudy, the Bank Group's resident representative in Mali

REVIEWING AND ASSESSING.
The villagers do their own monitoring and evaluations. The village committees, helped by the local nongovernmental organization, report how many people are involved, what training has been conducted, what is the level of satisfaction, and why. They also monitor whether behaviors such as hygiene, diet, and involvement in the committees have changed. Their information is aggregated by the local organization and consolidated at the national level. James D. Wolfensohn, president of the World Bank (at right in photo above), meets with the citizens of Korokoro, Mali, to learn about their experiences with the Grass-Roots Initiative project.

An estimated 200 villages are at the heart of the project, and about 130,000 people are expected to benefit. The training program will strengthen the skills and knowledge of 25 intermediary nongovernmental organizations, around 90 such organizations that work directly in community development, and more than 500 village animation agents. Close involvement with project execution will strengthen the organizational capacity and decision-making skills of village management committees. By its reliance on partnership, the project hopes to improve the collaboration between local technical services and regional and local development committees.

THE CHALLENGES AHEAD

Building sustainable partnerships is a delicate matter, requiring that everyone accept and fulfill his responsibilities if each partner is to benefit. As this project continues its partnership-building, there will no doubt be bumps along the way. The commitment of villagers to maintain the infrastructure they have built, long after the initial enthusiasm of project planning and implementation, will be a test of the project's philosophy. Finally, for continuing success, the commitment of the government to support future recurrent costs of village investments, such as teachers' salaries, has to be sustained. All of these challenges face the project's managers as they work toward long-term success.

The project is already making a difference at the local level and has been a useful testing ground for the decentralization that is in progress in Mali. The village committees supported by the project are receiving "on-the-job training" for the local decision making that the decentralization policy is trying to foster.
— Hasan Tuluy, country director

PROJECT TEAM

Adriana De Leva-task manager. Sidi Boubacar, Wolfgang Chadab, Abdoulaye Coulibaly, Chantal Dejou, Edmond Dembele, Francoise Genouille, Seydou Idani, Abdelghani Inal, Annick Lachance, Sekou Maiga, Carmen Malena, Linda McGinnis, Fatoumata Nafo-Traoré, Ok Pannenborg, Margaret Parlato, Jean Louis Sarbib, Richard Seifman, Antoine Simonpietri, Roger Sullivan, Serge Theunynck, Bourecima Touré, Cheick Traoré, Grace Yabrudy. Hasan Tuluy, country director.

Philippines

A PROSPERING NATION THIRSTS FOR CLEAN WATER

Despite impressive economic growth, public services in the sprawling archipelago of the Philippines have not kept up. Water and sanitation, in particular, are well behind what consumers want and are willing to pay for. Worst off are 1,000 small towns where water supplies are managed by municipal governments. These systems barely function.

THE TOWN OF MAGDALENA: THREE WATER SOURCES, NONE ADEQUATE
A typical case is the town of Magdalena, in the rolling hills of Laguna Province about 100 kilometers from Manila. The town has three water sources, none adequate: a stream, a municipal water supply system, and an 'informal' water supply system run by a community association. The water pressure is spotty, to say the least. People near the source get plenty of water while those at the end of the line get only a trickle.

The Magdalena municipal system, built in 1926, draws its water from a spring. The system has deteriorated to such an extent that each household is allowed to take water for only 45 minutes a day. Housewives at the far end of the system complain that they cannot even fill a pail in that amount of time.

In the town of Magdalena, in the Laguna Province of the Philippines, a historic cathedral (left) and an open air laundry (above) coexist within steps of one another. Lacking household water, the villagers wash their dishes and clothes in local streams and canals. The LGU (local government unit) Urban Water and Sanitation Project is changing this.

111

Until recently, water supply systems run by Philippine municipalities have been characterized by bad service and low public confidence. Engineers have drawn up designs without asking the consumers what they really want and are willing to pay for. A majority of residents have had to dig their own wells or buy water from vendors at exorbitant prices.

When we began the process of community consultations, we found that many people were willing to pay for the services which met their preferences for convenience, quality, and reliability—and thus, it became clear that the project would be able to attract the private sector to build and operate the systems.

— Vijay Jagannathan, task team leader.

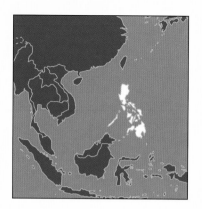

Overview

LOCAL GOVERNMENT UNIT URBAN WATER AND SANITATION PROJECT

A series of loans that will eventually bring water service to around a million people in small cities and towns. Each successive loan will be made based on the accomplishment of performance objectives under the previous loan.

Total financing: US$244.9 million

Bank Group contribution (Adjustable Program Loans, APL): APL I, 1999–2002, US$28 million; APL II, 2001–04, US$60 million; APL III, 2003–07, US$100 million

GOALS

Provide sanitary, accessible water to large towns with municipally managed systems.

Involve municipal government and communities in decision making; the go-ahead requires that at least 60 percent of local residents agree to the proposed service and tariff.

Involve the private sector in the investments.

Demonstrate that, with appropriate designs, pricing, and incentives, water supply systems, irrespective of size, can be made both viable and sustainable.

2007 TARGETS *

Give 90 percent of the urban population access to safe drinking water.

Collect and treat 80 percent of the wastewater in the 20 largest cities outside Manila.

PHILIPPINES AT A GLANCE

Population: 75 million

Land area: 298,000 sq. km.

GNP: US$78.9 billion

GNP per capita: US$1,050

Poverty: 28% (of population below national poverty line)

Urban population: 57% of total population

Life expectancy at birth: 68 years

Infant mortality: 35 per 1,000 live births

Child malnutrition: 30% (of children under 5)

Access to safe water: 83% (of total population)

Illiteracy: 5% (of population age 15 and older)

* See Appendix 1 for monitoring and evaluation information.

WATER USAGE. *A girl doing dishes at home (left). Notice the lack of plumbing. The red jug holds the water. The family may have good clothes, appliances, maybe a television. But household water connections are not yet standard for people who have won some of the other amenities of life. At the lower end of the Magdalena community, housewives complain that they waste almost half a day waiting for water. Rather than stand around, they leave a dishpan (below). When the water does come, the pan can overflow before it is retrieved. That's the reason for the puddle seen here, which creates a breeding ground for bacteria and disease.*

The only water treatment is haphazard cleaning and application of chlorine. The water is seldom tested, but a recent analysis showed it to be full of coliform, caused by contamination from a pigsty and seepage from septic tanks located along the leaky network.

MAGDALENA IS NOT ALONE

In 1998, virtually no one served by the other 1,000 municipal systems in the Philippines had water for more than a few hours a day. This dribble was often contaminated. Talk to any mother living in these towns, and she will tell you that her children are often sick from the filthy water. Although it is true that most people in the Philippines have access to medical attention, oral rehydration salts, and antibiotics, water-borne illnesses are common, especially among children. The country's infant mortality rate of 36 per thousand is the most telling evidence that something is not working.

SAFE, PLENTIFUL WATER

In the early 1990s, a review of the World Bank's portfolio reported that, in 1991, 43 percent of the water and sanitation sector's projects had major problems by the fourth or fifth year of implementation. Since then, many Bank staff have intensified their efforts to develop more effective projects. The Philippines Water and Sanitation Project, described here, is an example of the resulting innovations. The project is beginning to provide sanitary, accessible water to towns with municipally managed systems. Drawing from the first of three World Bank loans, the project covered 40 towns and about 155,000 people by 1999. The second and third loans—both World Bank Adaptable Program Loan instruments—will rapidly expand services, provided some basic performance triggers are attained.

ENTERPRISING WATER ASSOCIATION. *It's a myth that people are not willing to pay for water. The Barangay Water Supply Association serves one part of the town. A paid water vendor (above) maintains electric pumps and fills the jerry cans of the members. Members pay three cents (U.S.) for 18 to 20 liters.*

COMMUNITY CREATIVITY. *The same water supply association also maintains this big storage tank (right). Seventy-five lucky households fed by this tank have water taps inside their houses.*

The water and sanitation project's approach questions the traditional Filipino distinction between "viable" and "nonviable" water systems. Systems serving large cities and towns, where full economies of scale can be realized—reducing the cost to both investors and consumers—have been interpreted by policy makers to be "viable." These have generally been the main beneficiaries of development assistance. Small systems have, until now, been classified as "nonviable" and have had to rely on sporadic grants.

The project's philosophy is that, if communities can accept the idea that water and sanitation services should respond to what consumers want and are willing to pay for, any system can be viable. The project seeks to demonstrate that, with appropriate designs, pricing, and incentives, water supply systems, irrespective of size,

NOT VERY SANITARY. *This stream (below) comes from a spring. The water is used for bathing and laundry, and it also supplies the water for Calamba, a town near Magdalena.*

115

can pay for themselves. The ultimate test of viability will be the willingness of the private sector to participate in the needed investments.

The project team, in consultation with local officials, first estimated the amounts the municipalities were capable of and willing to borrow. Typically, the borrowing capacity was between US$800,000 and US$1 million. Technical consultants thereafter surveyed the physical conditions and proposed technical options that could be financed within each town's budget envelope. Then the townspeople were consulted, in order to elicit what type of service they wanted and how much they were willing to pay. If at least 60 percent of the community indicated a desire for one of the feasible options, a detailed design was drawn up for their approval.

ATTRACTING THE PRIVATE SECTOR

The project is promoting public-private partnerships in the delivery of services. In this arrangement, the local government bears the investment risks but leases out the constructed facilities to the private sector on a 15-year lease contract. Magdalena is the first municipality to have concluded such a lease contract. The concept will be proved beyond a doubt if the private sector is willing to invest time, effort, and money in water supply services in several more project towns.

LOAN PHASES: WATER FOR A MILLION PEOPLE

This is the World Bank's first water supply project using the Adaptable Program Loan (APL) instrument. This type of loan gives borrowers flexibility to test innovative designs through relatively small operations, monitor and evaluate the lessons, and then scale up to a sufficient size. Each successive loan will be made based on the accomplishment of performance objectives under the previous loan.

APL I: Test the concept in about 35 municipalities, with 35,000 new service connections.

APL II: If the arrangements for commercial operation, management, and revenue collection made during the first loan prove satis-

MUNICIPAL COUNCIL MEETING.

The project's preparation has involved extensive consultations. Once a mayor expresses interest, the project team undertakes a financial analysis to assess the amount the municipality could afford to borrow and whether it is in a position to provide the required equity of 10 percent. Subsequently, the engineering team surveys and evaluates the technical options that are feasible within the available budget. The options, along with costs and implications for service levels, are presented to the mayor, municipal

councils and communities. At the community level, at least 60 percent need to agree to the proposed service and tariff.

Above: Magdalena's mayor, Pablo Agapay, fourth from right, and a representative from the Department of Interior and Local Government explain the water project to the municipal council. After more consultations, the council approves the project.

116

factory, the second loan will provide for a scale-up to around 80 additional cities and municipalities.

Requirements for expanding to APL III: Satisfactory financial performance in the 80 water utilities receiving financing under APL II. The utilities must also provide connections for at least 60 percent of households in any participating barangay (village) and at least 16 hours of water per day to participating households. The utilities must also demonstrate that an average of 80 percent of consumers are satisfied with service performance.

APL III: Induce private-sector banks to invest in approximately 130 more municipal utilities for water supply and sanitation, with the Development Bank of the Philippines serving these banks as a wholesaler of the investments. This will bring the total customers served to at least a million.

RESULTS SO FAR

As of mid-1999, in 12 municipalities, between 65 and 70 percent of the residents had signed willingness-to-connect forms. More than 250 towns had signed letters of intent to borrow money to finance their water systems. Ten towns were starting construction of their systems. In another 19, project preparation was under way. The first system was to be completed by fall 2000.

"In virtually any country," says Vijay Jagannathan, World Bank team leader, "there is moral suasion at the local level. Information is available and citizens know what is happening. If the chief of your village has something you don't have, you start asking questions.

"As a male," he says, "I must observe that, if you put a woman in charge, you seldom get a case where she steals. Women are often more concerned with the community's welfare than with their own immediate gain. They are also the ones who are most affected by things not working out. Of course, the project works with men, but we do make a special effort to involve women in the decision making."

By decentralizing, the project managers hope to ensure accountability. But the World Bank's water sector projects have stumbled in the past. "The Philippines Water and Sanitation project is a pilot," Mr. Jagannathan concludes. "We shouldn't claim victory when we are only starting. Let's monitor it and see if it works out. That's the idea of an Adaptable Program Loan."

PROJECT TEAM

Vijay Jagannathan, task team leader. Luiz Claudio Tavares, Aldo Baietti, George Calderon, Harvey Garn, Karen Jonesy Jacob, Karen Hudes, Hoi-Chan Nguyen, Mariles Navarro, Martha Ochieng, Heinrich Unger, Cecilia Vales, Albert Wright, Vinay K. Bhargava, country directors. Keshav Varma, sector director.

CONSENSUS BUILDING. *Magdalena's Mayor Agapay consulted with water customers. With the assistance of a local project team, he explained the design options and the corresponding prices. Then there were more meetings and house-to-house visits. The householders decided, and they signed up for the water project.*

On May 31, 1999, a private operator, Benpres Holding Co., won the bid for the Magdalena water system on a 15-year lease contract. The mayor (left) has cause to celebrate. He is confident his constituents' water problems will soon be over.

Estonia

A BREATH OF FRESH AIR IN THE BALTIC

Asthma. Clothes that never would get clean. Buildings with their paint shredded by the acrid dust. The gray town was topped by a gray cloud and surrounded 40 kilometers in every direction by gray farms, beaches, and hills. "I drove to Estonia from Denmark for the first time right after independence," says Niels Vestergaard, International Finance Corporation senior environmental specialist. "It is no exaggeration to say that all the color had disappeared. The town was totally gray. And no wonder: The dust cloud could easily be seen as far away as 20 kilometers."

This was Kunda, Estonia, population 5,000, where everyone was choking on the same gray dust, as much as 129,000 tons of it a year, from the government's Kunda Cement Plant. One of many polluters across the former Soviet Union and one of the worst in Estonia, the plant belched out one-third of the country's particulate emissions.

The community protested. Even though the company was the town's major employer, people tried to get the town council to shut the plant down. The citizens of Finland, Sweden, and Norway didn't like the sulfuric acid and nitrogen dioxide emissions wafting their way either.

Kunda, Estonia, before and after—dismal and colorless under a cloud of dust (opposite). The people complained about respiratory problems and often wore masks in order to filter the air. Renovating the factory reduced emissions by more than 98 percent and refreshed every aspect of life. After the cement factory cleanup (above) farms prospered, and the city became green.

Overview

Privatization, modernization, and cleanup of Estonia's only cement company. Construction of a major port.

Total financing: US$48 million; Bank Group (International Finance Corporation) contribution: US$6 million loan and US$4 million equity

Partners: Atlas Nordic Cement, Government of Estonia, Nordic Environmental Finance Corporation, Finnish Fund for Industrial Cooperation Ltd. (FINNFUND)

GOALS

Reduce polluting emissions by more than 98.5 percent.

Modernize the company and increase its sales, both domestic and international.

Eliminate trucking the cement to a port 100 kilometers away.

See hell while it lasts.

— *1993 Estonian guidebook describing Kunda.*

IMPACT

Reduced emission of dust by 1,240 tons per year—more than 98.5 percent.

Reduced unemployment to .7 percent in 1998 and 1999, compared with the country's unemployment rate of 10 percent.

Saved US$372,000 per year in treatment costs and days lost from work due to respiratory diseases.

ESTONIA AT A GLANCE

Population: 1.4 million

Land area: 42,000 sq km

GNP: US$4.9 billion

GNP per capita: US$3,390

Poverty: 9%
(of population below national poverty line)

Urban population: 74%
of total population

Life expectancy at birth: 70 years

Infant mortality: 10 per 1,000 live births

Child malnutrition:
Not available

Access to safe water: 79%
(of total population)

Illiteracy: 4%
(of population age 15 and older)

Kunda Cement, itself gasping for life, was hopelessly dirty and outmoded, with 15 percent of its annual production going up in dust. If it was not to be closed, it needed mouth-to-mouth resuscitation.

In 1992, Estonia, population 1.5 million, had just gained independence from the crumbling Soviet Union and was rushing to modernize. But people in Kunda were being left behind.

THE SILVER LINING

As part of its program to privatize state-owned companies, the government had sold off 35 percent of Kunda Cement; but the company needed more funds for its rejuvenation. The company had low production costs, access to cheap raw materials, a great location on the Baltic, near Helsinki and St. Petersburg—and it was the only cement company in the country. The circumstances made it a good candidate for investment by the Bank Group's International Finance Corporation (IFC).

It is very important to me that, after Estonia had regained its independence, IFC so quickly found the way to this most desolate industrial area and transformed it. The Kunda success gave people confidence that industrial development does not necessarily mean enormous environmental sacrifices.
— Mart Laar, Prime Minister of Estonia

Just as we were preparing for the ceremonies to open the new Kunda port, an old cement filter, and the building it was in, exploded. Someone, perhaps deliberately, had dropped a tire into it. The citizens in the region wanted to close the plant immediately, and they made this loudly known to all the dignitaries attending the ceremony. The sponsors were ready to cancel the celebrations and reconsider their long-term investment.

But the Estonian Minister of Environment pointed to the mess and said, "Now you see why we have to fix this place up!" His intervention saved the day.
— Jyrki Koskelo,
Chief Investment Officer, IFC

Collapsed factory building (right) after cement filter exploded.

The IFC puts together investment deals in the developing countries and provides the technical assistance needed for a successful outcome. To assist Estonia's modernization, the IFC was interested in businesses that could boost exports.

To breathe new life into Kunda Cement, the IFC helped foreign sponsors and the government to work out a major modernization and cleanup. The company committed to get rid of the plant's emissions. The investors also decided to build a port to avoid having to truck the cement 100 kilometers to the port in Talinn.

VENTURE IN JEOPARDY

Two days before the ribbon cutting ceremony of the new Kunda port, with all the dignitaries coming, the only remaining old cement filter blew up. A very large building filled with thousands of tons of cement dust exploded and collapsed. A mushroom cloud—like a nuclear explosion—could be seen over tens of miles. This caused a vehement public reaction against Kunda Cement. Fortunately, the officials were able to calm the situation, and the company survived.

Although Estonians were relatively prosperous, healthy, and well-educated compared with people in most of the World Bank's borrowing members, the country was recovering from the collapse of its socialist system. The Bank Group committed to help promote economic growth and improve living standards.
— Jemal-ud-din-Kassum,
vice president, investment operations,
International Finance Corporation

Ten years ago, this was a closed Soviet military zone with no port. Now it is a major exporting center.
— Leho Valimae, truck driver whose logs are being off-loaded.

One-quarter of the country's wood exports now move through Kunda. Previously, they had to be trucked to a port 100 kilometers away.

124

With the renovations, the company was able to reduce emissions by 98.5 percent. The US$8 million investment in environmental improvement showed an economic rate of return of 25 percent—in other words, a US$2 million bonus to the larger community. The people now benefit from new services, such as transport and auto repair; improved yield of the farms immediately around the plant; clean clothes, buildings, and cars; a reduction in respiratory diseases; and higher real estate values. Even Estonia's neighbors—in Latvia and Lithuania and parts of Finland, Sweden, Norway, Russia, Belarus, and Poland—are breathing better.

By 1997, Estonian cement consumption had skyrocketed by 41 percent and, in 1998, by another 27 percent—all from local demand. Even larger demand was coming from Finland, Latvia, Lithuania, Russia, Poland, Germany, Portugal, and West Africa.

The surge in business has brought 200 new jobs into the area with higher wages and salaries. The factory's average wage increased from around US$50 a month in 1992 to US$500 a month in 1999. This is about 15 percent higher than the national average. In addition, the company spends US$3 million a year on local services. In 1999, unemployment in Kunda was less than 1 percent as compared with 10 percent for the country as a whole.

These achievements smoothed the way for the final stage of privatization. By spring 1999, one of the original investors had purchased the government's remaining shares.

The new port of Kunda has been a dramatic and unpredicted success. The port is close to Estonia's manufacturing centers and to Baltic markets. Although it was built to serve the cement company, 75 percent of its shipping is now from other businesses.

Look at these sparkling windows! Before, you had to clean them with acid water to prevent cement from etching itself into the glass.
— *Tiiu Raju, town museum keeper*

Buildings and cars stay cleaner now. Above: the town museum with its spotless windows. Opposite: The small farms adjacent to the plant have flourished. Yields are estimated to have increased by 10 percent a year.

THE KUNDA MODEL

The early accomplishments in Kunda energized Estonia's reforms as the country dismantled its socialist institutions and built a market economy. The overhaul of the country's environmental and commercial laws was based on the lessons learned from Kunda. More foreign investors came in, mainly from Finland and Sweden. The new investments are responsible for a large portion of Estonia's exports.

Kunda gave the government the confidence and experience needed to make additional privatizations a lot easier, and these proceeded very quickly. In 1996, the World Bank reported that the Estonians had privatized more than 400 medium-size and large industrial firms, and 1,100 small businesses. The Bank said that, in scope and pace, Estonian privatization had been a success. No privatized firm had failed, and most divested firms were expanding their employment.

THE COMPANY'S FUTURE

At the end of the nineties, the IFC was invited to put together a new deal. The original Kunda partners decided to invest in a cogeneration plant to provide electricity for Kunda Cement and heat for the city of Kunda. This would allow the city to close the current district heating plant, the only remaining polluter in the region. The project is also doubling or tripling the port's cargo capacity and providing room for other industries to grow.

PROJECT TEAM

Jyrki Koskelo, chief investment officer. Esteban Altschul, Kenneth Assal, John Beale, Claudio Bonnefoy, Lance Christ, Milana Gorshkova, George Gouda, Assaad Jabre, Willfried Keffenberger, Caroline Kahn, Marge Karner, D. Keesing, Kristen Klemperer, George Konda, Natalie Matushenko, Mohan Pherwani, Brian Pinto, Richard Ranken, Zimie Rim, Niels Vestergaard, Andrus Viirg, Edward Nassim and Harold Rosen, directors.

Kunda is typical of Estonia's overall progress. In 1997, the country's privatizations, market reforms, fiscal and monetary policies, and a liberal free trade regime resulted in GDP growth of 10 percent and a drop in inflation to 11 percent. Continued growth is forecasted. Estonia was among the first group of central European countries identified for accession to the European Union. Companies such as Kunda are contributing to the development of local economies and supporting the growth of the country as a whole.

— Harold Rosen, director, central and southern Europe, IFC

Bolivia

BEYOND THE GOLD RUSH:
WHAT CORPORATE CITIZENSHIP CAN DO

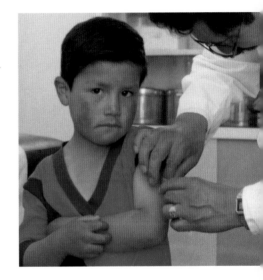

The Inti Raymi Foundation has invested US$5 million on education, health care, animal husbandry, small construction projects, and local businesses such as crafts (opposite). Above: Getting ready for an inoculation at the Chiquiña health center, staffed by the Inti Raymi Foundation.

The Bolivian altiplano is a vast steppe land, almost 12,000 feet high, which stretches between the Peruvian and Argentine borders. This dry and hostile plateau formed part of the lands of the ancient Incas. At their most important festival, called Inti Raymi, the Incas celebrated the winter solstice in honor of the sun, which they worshipped. As part of their festival, they sacrificed a white llama in hopes of a good harvest. A modern-day namesake of the sun god's festival is a huge gold mine at Kori Kollo on the altiplano. The Inti Raymi mine is the most important in Bolivia and the largest employer in the Oruro district. In 1991, Inti Raymi was seeking to expand and looking for investors. At a time when Bolivia was a risky country for foreign investment, the World Bank Group's International Finance Corporation (IFC) helped finance the mine's expansion as well as new production technology and infrastructure. Production increased dramatically.

The expanded Inti Raymi Company has had a major impact on the economy of the district, beginning with an entire new town. All 135 new houses have electricity, potable water, and sewerage. The village has a new school, a church, a health center, a municipal building, and a market.

129

Oh, lift your head to the

dying sun

And, on bended knees,

listening to the dreadful

Prayer for mercy of

the wind of the high

plateau,

Hope that, on the altar of

the snow,

The immaterial priest

raises

The Eucharist in the

shape of the moon.

—from "The Llama," by Gregorio Reynolds

Overview

INTI RAYMI FOUNDATION

Foundation established by the Inti Raymi company, operator of the largest gold mine in Bolivia, to promote local development. The foundation has spent about US$5 million on social programs in the 25 communities the area.

GOALS

Promote education, improve health care, and modernize livestock production.

Contribute to community infrastructure and promote handicraft businesses.

BOLIVIA AT A GLANCE

Population: 7.9 million

Land area: 1,084,000 sq km

GNP: US$7.9 billion

GNP per capita: US$1,000

Poverty: 67%
(of population below national poverty line)

Urban population: 63% of total population

Life expectancy at birth:
62 years

Infant mortality:
67 per 1,000 live births

Child malnutrition: 9%
(of children under 5)

Access to safe water: 60%
(of total population)

Illiteracy: 17%
(of population age 15 and older)

Health care. *The foundation provides primary health care at a clinic in the town of Chiquiña, and also has a program of preventive health care for 5,000 inhabitants of the 25 communities around the mine operation.*

The mine has generated 700 jobs and spends US$8.2 million per year in salaries and benefits. It also spends US$18 million annually on local goods and services and pays US$4 million in taxes.

At the same time, both to earn a "local license" to operate and as an expression of corporate concern, the company created the Inti Raymi Foundation to promote local development. The IFC encourages its corporate clients to form local ties with the communities where they operate. It has drawn upon the Inti Raymi experience when providing consultation about community relations programs.

The company has financed about US$5 million of foundation spending on social programs in 25 area communities, often leveraging its resources through joint projects with local governments and other foundations. Activities are concentrated in education, health care, and livestock, with additional contributions to infrastructure and crafts.

The late Mario Mercado Vaca
Guzman, founder and president of
both the Inti Raymi Company and
the Inti Raymi Foundation, New
Villa Chuquiña.

In the Oruro enrichment center, above.
Schools in the city of Oruro, 40 kilometers from the mine, often lack sanitation, textbooks, computers, and
sports fields. So the Inti Raymi Foundation built an enrichment center,
with a library, 20 computers, a gym,
art studios, sports fields, and a
playroom. The city's 28 schools now
send as many as 1,000 children a day
to the center.

Together with the government, the
foundation has financed the construction of 10 new schools around the mine
and helps maintain and improve
existing schools. The foundation also
pays for school breakfast and lunch
programs.

Celebrating the arrival of electricity
(right). The city government had
US$15,000. The prefecture had
US$97,500. But electric power would
cost much more than that. The Inti
Raymi Foundation brought together
the Inter-American Foundation of
the United States, the local governments, and the people. Jointly, the
donors contributed US$30,000. Local
citizens contributed US$7500. And
now, nine communities are connected
to the grid.

Below: One of 500 pumps installed with the foundation's help—one feature of the expanded water supplies and training that residents receive to operate and maintain their own system.

Science class at the Oruro Enrichment Center (above right).

The lands of the Bolivian altiplano are harsh and arid. With cropland limited, sheep herding (right) is a main source of income. The Inti Raymi Foundation has supported this business by introducing improvements in animal husbandry.

In addition to its social contributions, the Inti Raymi company has had to deal with a number of environmental issues common to the mining industry. These include air and water quality, mining and industrial wastes, dam safety, and land reclamation.

The company is adequately addressing these issues and is currently in compliance with both Bolivian regulations and IFC/World Bank policies and guidelines.

IFC reviews the social and environmental impacts of projects and, by drawing on the experiences of leading companies, helps to come up with advice and solutions. We have learned a great deal from the Inti Raymi experience, which we have been able to share with other companies.
—Philippe Lietard, director, IFC oil, gas, and mining department

THE FUTURE

Inti Raymi Foundation has been grappling with two related issues: long-term funding and the sustainability of its management, programs, and policies.

Funding appears the lesser problem. The Inti Raymi Company is developing additional mining operations in the area and may extend its involvement in the foundation. However, that involvement will not go on forever, and the foundation leadership has a commitment to wean itself from company support. This seems possible: Inti Raymi is establishing a subsidiary foundation in the United States to raise funds in the form of both loans and matching grants.

Foundation management has also been an issue. At first it was difficult to retain qualified staff because these professionals were being recruited from La Paz. This problem was resolved when the foundation started hiring personnel from the Oruro region where there was a large cadre of eligible professionals.

Inti Raymi was ahead of the trend in building a foundation, partnering with others, and promoting local development. Companies throughout Latin America, in India, the Philippines, South Africa, and elsewhere are following suit.
—Waldemar Maj, senior investment officer, IFC oil, gas, and mining department

PROJECT TEAM

John Barton-Bridges, Jean-Claude Goldbrenner, Waldemar Maj, Hung Nguyen, investment officers. Clive Armstrong, Mauricio Athiée, Jean-Michel Attlan, Sabina Beg, Nicole Bolster, Lawrence Bouton, Robert Brown, Louise Renee Dankerlin, Sakdiyiam Kupasrimonkol, Claus Westmeier. Philippe Liétard, director, IFC oil, gas and mining department. Azmat Taufique, manager, IFC mining division.

Argentina

This two-part chapter highlights the programs Argentina has undertaken, with World Bank Group help, to target social services to those in need.

Argentina entered the 20th century one of the richest countries in the world. In 1910, the country ranked ahead of the United States and Great Britain and was only slightly behind France in terms of per capita gold reserves. But Argentina spent most of the next 80 years going downhill. In the 1970s, inflation became a constant. At one point, it reached 200 percent a month. Coming into the 1990s, Argentina was on the brink of bankruptcy. But then, in a very short period of time, this country of 35 million people underwent a remarkable economic transformation, reaching a GNP of US$8,970 per capita—more than double the average of other Latin American nations.

The prosperity arose out of far-reaching reforms undertaken during the 1990s. In 1991, the government tied the peso one-to-one to the dollar, and outlawed the printing of money to finance deficit spending. This was the first of many reforms—among them, mass privatizations, debt restructuring, trade deregulation, reform of the financial sector, a new tax system, and a streamlined civil service. These have laid the foundation for a modern, prosperous country.

Although many people remember Argentina as having a first class education system (producing Nobel prize winners in medicine, chemistry, and mathematics), education has suffered from decades of under-investment and stagnation. This has resulted in a growing education gap between the rich and poor.

Overview

Most of the new wealth fell into the hands of an already rich elite. The gap between rich and poor widened in virtually every nation that embraced reform [Argentina included].... Many Latin Americans trapped in poverty by reforms fail to see the light because they can only feel the pain ... the losers sit in anguish, watching their lives fall apart in a globalization purgatory.

— Anthony Faiola, Washington Post, December 8, 1999

The PROMIN Project is helping to build and improve primary health care centers, child feeding centers, and kindergartens. It is working to bring early child development and pediatric, maternal, and prenatal health care up to Western standards.

Total cost: US$330 million; World Bank (IBRD) program loans, US$200 million
External partners: United Nations Development Programme, UNICEF

PROMIN II GOALS

As an expansion of PROMIN I, PROMIN II's main goals are to reduce the proportion of underweight babies, reduce the proportion of malnourished pregnant women, and reduce the proportion of children up to five years who are malnourished. Client satisfaction will be a significant measure of the project's success.

PROMIN II TARGETS *

Reduce the proportion of underweight babies by 70 percent.
Reduce the proportion of malnourished pregnant women by 30 percent.
Reduce the proportion of malnourished children up to age five by 50 percent.
Increase the share of women receiving maternal and prenatal care by 60 percent.
Increase the share of children up to age six receiving health care by 60 percent.
Increase the proportion of children fully vaccinated by 80 percent.

ARGENTINA AT A GLANCE

Population: 36.1 million

Land area: 2,737,000 sq km

GNP: US$324.1 billion

GNP per capita: US$8,970

Poverty: Not available

Urban population:
89% (of total population)

Life expectancy at birth: 73 years

Infant mortality: 22 per 1,000
live births

Child malnutrition:
2% (of children under 5)

Access to safe water:
65% (of total population)

Illiteracy: 4% (of population
age 15 and older)

* See Appendix 1 for monitoring and evaluation information.

Nevertheless, Argentina suffered a severe recession during 1995, with unemployment reaching almost 19 percent—or 6.5 million people. After a breather, in 1998 the nation was back in recession again and stayed there for the rest of the decade. Besides a jolt from the Asia crisis, one of the chief reasons for the downturn was the 40 percent devaluation of the Brazilian cruzeiro in early 1999, which made Argentina's products way too expensive for the Brazilian market. Autos and other exports were seriously hurt.

Prohibited by law from printing money and spending its way out of the downturn, the government had few short-term options and ended the century with unemployment hovering at around 15 percent.

Among ordinary Argentines, the hardest hit are those over 45 years old, with obsolete skills, and youth trying to enter a highly demanding labor market.

With the opening up of the economy, employers demand increasing levels of skills and education. Myrna Alexander, World Bank country director for Argentina, says, "Now it seems that even a secondary education may not be enough to command a decent salary, and the trend in high dropout rates for the poor is making income disparities worse: Income for the skilled has grown, while those without skills have lost income."

SOCIAL PROGRAMS

Many of the world's wealthiest nations are fighting deficits and taxes by cutting their social programs. Despite recessions and budget woes, Argentina has been going in the opposite direction: As finances, budgets, taxes and administration modernize, the government has been able to expand public services and help to the poor. During the 1990s, Argentina steadily increased its public social expenditures to US$52 billion or 16.5 percent of gross domestic product. The nation spends US$19 billion on social security. Federal spending of US$6 billion on health and education is augmented by US$16 billion in provincial outlays.

About 1.5 million of Argentina's children live in shanties with poor hygiene and poor access to health care.

"Before, almost everyone had permanent jobs. [Now,] we don't have work and we don't have food for our families."

"Yes, it's clear; that's the way things are—little work, badly paid."

"We used to be united. Now we kill each other."

"I don't believe it's going to get better. It's going to get worse."

—Argentina: Consultations with the Poor, *World Bank, 1999.*

We are helping Argentina bring its health care up to the level of a developed country—which Argentina is. Still more improvements are needed in primary health care. In the future, Argentina will introduce health insurance for the poor. This will fill a very significant gap in social services. When the insurance scheme is piloted, incentives will be tested to encourage people to use clinics instead of hospitals when appropriate. In addition, the pilot will try out financial incentives to encourage health center staff to go out into the neighborhoods and reach children and mothers who rarely come to the health centers.

—Marie-Odile Waty, task manager

Argentina is not an "IDA country." That is, it is not poor enough to qualify for the low-interest loans provided by the Bank Group's International Development Agency (IDA). And the World Bank's investments there are relatively small compared with the size of the overall economy and government budget. The loans described here, comparable in terms to commercial credits, come from the International Bank for Reconstruction and Development (IBRD). (See Appendix III, *The World Bank Group,* for details about the Bank Group's institutions.) Investments in human capital, particularly education, health and social protection, have been a major part of the Bank's program in Argentina since 1993.

Argentina has a doctor-to-population ratio among the highest in Latin America. It has an extensive health system. But, until recently, health spending has focused on medical insurance for the elderly and for workers in the formal, private sector. The long-term jobless have no health insurance and have to depend on public hospitals for most care.

Hospitals are free for the poor. But, over the past few years as a result of the economic crisis, the hospitals have been jammed, and waiting lines are long. People have had nowhere else to turn, either because they have lost their jobs and their company-paid health insurance or because, although still employed, they cannot afford the co-payments required by their company's insurance. Public health services are poorly equipped to handle the growing demand. This is especially true of primary care services and prevention, which have never had adequate resources.

With a high need for health care, poor mothers and children have suffered disproportionately. The Health, Nutrition, and Early Childhood Development Project is designed to support Argentina in providing first-class health and child care for these disadvantaged children and mothers.

This child development center in an Argentina shantytown (left) is typical of the quality the country is seeking for its poorest and youngest citizens.

We have had a core team working together for years, and we work very closely with the resident mission. Humor is one of our strengths.
— Marian Kaminskis, staff assistant.

THE PROJECT

To help impoverished children and their mothers and following the latest early childhood development methods, the government is building and upgrading primary health care centers, child feeding centers, and kindergartens and bringing pediatric, maternal, and prenatal health care up to developed country standards. The World Bank, United Nations Development Programme, and UNICEF are providing support to the project, which is called PROMIN.

Having begun on a smaller scale (PROMIN I), by the end of the 1990s, PROMIN II was operating in more than 20 municipalities, each with a poverty rate of at least 30 percent. The World Bank supported-program reaches almost 1.8 million people. In addition, a number of local governments are using their own resources to extend the PROMIN model to other areas.

PROMIN complements other Bank-financed health reforms in the hospital, public health, and health insurance sectors.

WHAT MAKES THE NEW APPROACH WORK

New information systems are key to smooth operations. The systems make it easy to provide holistic care via a set program of appointments, check regularly whether needed care has been received, track patients' medical history, organize an efficient flow of patients through the clinic, closely monitor groups at risk, and improve referral and counter-referral systems.

PROMIN PROJECT TEAM

Evangeline Javier, Marie Odile Waty, Jean-Jacques de St. Antoine, task managers. Girindre Beeharry, Luis Fara (project coordinator), Robert Pagano, Fernando Abadie, Enrique Abeya, Marta Capuccio, Victor Farías, María Laura Barral, Mario Bibiloni, Alexander Abrantes, Dr. Fernando Vio, Christian Hurtado, Marian Kaminskis, Patricia Bernedo, James Cercone, Orville Grimes, Ferenc Molnar, Clemencia Onesty, Morag Van Praag, Rudy Van Puymbroeck. Myrna Alexander, country director.

HIGH STANDARD FACILITIES. *Children play with a construction kit (top), one of many learning activities and toys made available to them.*

Volunteer mothers in uniforms (above) work in the kitchen. Wholesome food and meals are planned by nutritionists who instruct the children and mothers in healthy eating

The project targets poor women and children, the most vulnerable groups, in a period of economic difficulty. Technically, it is well designed. It focuses on monitoring and improving quality and efficiency and benefits from a highly motivated and competent Argentinean team.
— Jean Jacques de St. Antoine, *former task manager*

HEALTH CENTERS. *Gone are the long lines. In the past, patients just showed up—and waited. Now they make appointments to see a doctor or a nurse. These health centers and the way they are run have brought about a radical change in the quality of care, according to patient feedback. The attending staff show professional pride and observe the set schedules.*

We need to stop this fiesta for the few.

—campaign slogan from the 1999 Argentine elections.

rgentina's economic shock therapy and recessions have really hurt people and not only those who lack the skills, education and flexibility to participate in a modern economy. For the past 20 years, unemployment in Argentina has been growing. In 1980, it was almost nonexistent at 2 percent, but through the 1980s, it grew to about 8 percent and peaked at 18 percent in 1995. Twenty-nine percent of urban Argentinians fall below the country's poverty line.

Although the government spends about $400 million annually on unemployment insurance, the benefits to someone who loses a job last for 12 months. Farmers, the self-employed, and odd-job workers do not pay social security and therefore do not receive unemployment benefits. To provide temporary work, the government has established the TRABAJAR (work) program, with the double advantage of giving the poor a modest safety net and helping to build much-needed public facilities, such as basic water and sanitation, small roads and community kitchens. A series of World Bank credits have helped to finance TRABAJAR.

The project targets the poorest people in the country, including those with minimal skills. The targeting mechanism is simple: TRABAJAR's wages are kept low enough to be attractive only to those who have few job prospects.

The program is managed by the Ministry of Labor and Social Security. But the real action takes place at the local level, where subprojects are initiated by municipalities and private organizations. School construction and repair, basic sanitation, small roads, bridges, health centers, community kitchens, and low-cost housing are all possibilities. The sub-projects must demonstrate sound engineering, costs, and plans for maintenance. Beyond this, the most important criterion for obtaining approval is the poverty level of the location. Once under way, the sub-projects must be completed within three to six months. Generally, the sponsoring agency funds the cost of materials and any skilled labor, and TRABAJAR finances the wages of unskilled labor up to a maximum of US$200 per month per worker for six months. Some 650,000 temporary jobs have been generated. TRABAJAR targets the poorest of the poor.

The comforts of home in Buenos Aires (opposite): cardboard walls, dirt floor, zinc roof, homemade furniture, battered cabinet, stove, refrigerator, and clock. In Argentina, even most poor people own refrigerators, television sets, and washing machines. Virtually everyone has electricity.

145

The TRABAJAR project has provided temporary work and supported small sub-projects in needy urban and rural communities all over the country. Municipalities and private organizations initiate the sub-projects, which are reviewed and approved by regional committees.

The committee members include government employment and training managers; someone from the national office of the Ministry of Labor and Social Security; and civil society observers, mostly business and union representatives.

The sub-projects—such as water and sanitation, small roads, schools, child care centers, and community kitchens— are basic and simple. To be selected, they must demonstrate technical, economic, financial, institutional, environmental, and social feasibility. Pictured here: Workers in Buenos Aires (above left and right) and, in San Juan (opposite), a group of workers passing buckets of concrete to the roof of a school being constructed.

Over time, it has become clear that very poor municipalities have little

ability to prepare and execute sub-projects or pay for the materials. So, in 300 poor municipalities, for works under US$35,000 total, TRABAJAR is now covering up to US$20,000 of materials and giving more technical assistance.

SOCIAL PROTECTION PROJECTS II AND III (TRABAJAR)

TRABAJAR helps the jobless poor by providing temporary employment on local public works projects initiated by municipalities and private nonprofit organizations.

Total financing: project II, US$1.2 billion, project III, US$1.1 billion
Bank Group contribution: project II, US$200 million; project III, US$284 million

GOALS

Give the unemployed poor a safety net by providing temporary, paid work.

Build public facilities, such as basic water and sanitation, small roads, and community kitchens.

ACHIEVEMENTS FROM MAY 1997 TO NOVEMBER 1999

650,000 temporary jobs.

US$200 per month per worker over five months on average.

80 percent of the workers were in the poorest 20 percent of the population, with more than half from the bottom 10 percent.

The facts support the bitter complaints Argentines made in *Argentina: Consultations with the Poor,* (World Bank, 1999). It is true that unemployment is very high, and poverty has increased. TRABAJAR provides only short-term relief and affects only around one-fifth of the unemployed. The long-term work prospects for many people are not good. They are short on marketable education and skills.

A complicating factor is the strength of the unions. Myrna Alexander points out that the unions are powerful enough in Argentina to maintain inflexible wages and generous benefits (such as family allowances). All companies, large and small, are required to comply with nationally negotiated labor agreements that establish national pay scales and benefits. Although workers pay as much as 20 percent of their earnings for these benefits, Argentina's compensation rates put pressure on Argentina's worldwide competitiveness. "There is a disincentive to large companies to hire new employees," Alexander says, "and this has led many small and medium-sized firms to avoid paying the benefits by hiring off the books, or *en negro.* These workers are most at risk of being laid off, because they are not registered and do not receive social security. It is estimated that some 40 to 45 percent of the total labor force is now paid *en negro.*"

Thus, there are jobs for the unskilled. In fact, 60 to 70 percent of the poor actually work. Unskilled labor pays around US$4,500 a year—generous compared with other Latin American countries—but not enough to keep a family of five or more above the poverty line.

Ms. Alexander continues, "It is not easy to persuade people that high wages and inflexible labor regulations are an obstacle to employment. Nevertheless, the Bank Group has recommended that the government take the politically difficult step of introducing greater flexibility in labor negotiations."

"But equally important," she says, "are programs to promote social equity—education, health insurance, and work programs such as TRABAJAR . During an economic crisis, when the need is

In a survey of TRABAJAR *ditch diggers in Formosa Province, the workers indicated high appreciation for the opportunity to earn some money. The program has been evaluated through two household surveys.*

Argentina is a bellwether for the success of market economy initiatives in Latin America and elsewhere. In the long run, in order to take care of its citizens and maintain political support for a liberalized economy Argentina, already ahead of many middle income countries in its social programs, is going to have to make a much greater commitment to promoting social equity, particularly through education, health insurance, unemployment insurance, and work programs such as TRABAJAR*. During an economic crisis when the need is greater and tax revenues fall off, such a commitment is much more difficult to maintain. To cope with such emergencies in the future, the government of Argentina is required by a new law to establish a fiscal surplus by 2003 and set funds aside to cover downturns.*

—Myrna Alexander, World Bank country director

Left: Claudia Berra, project coordinator from the Ministry of Labor, and the mayor of San Antonio, Juyjuy, a beautiful little mountain town, visit a school being built by TRABAJAR *workers.*

*From May, 1997 to November, 1999 30,000 sub-projects were approved, creating about 650,000 temporary jobs.
— Claudia Berra.*

greater and tax revenues fall off, such a commitment is much more difficult to maintain. It can be done. In 1999, we worked with the government to ensure that some US$980 million in federal government spending for targeted social programs was kept, despite the fact that the overall budget had to fall. In addition, many of the provinces, which have the primary responsibility for health and education, were able to keep up the commitment by cutting waste."

"Finally," Ms. Alexander says, "the poor tend to have more children than the rich, which, unfortunately, results in some 43 percent of children in Argentina living below the poverty line. This adds to the urgency of health and education programs such as PROMIN but also points to a great need for more aggressive action in the area of family planning."

Argentina is attempting to maintain equilibrium in liberalizing its economy, carrying out sound fiscal and budgetary practices, and taking care of its poor. The country brings much greater wealth to bear than many countries can. But the political and social dilemmas are still there. These two chapters illustrate the complexities of such a balancing act.

PROJECT TEAM

Polly Jones, task manager. Sandra Cesilini, Jean-Jacques de St. Antoine, Armando Godinez, Margaret Grosh, Christian Hurtado, Ruth Izquierdo, Jyotsna Jalan, Karla McEvoy, Rudy Van Puymbroeck, Morag Van Praag, Martin Ravallion, Maria Claudia Vasquez. Myrna Alexander, country director.

Colombia

BEAUTY, VIOLENCE, AND HOPE

Equal in size to Portugal, Spain, and France together, and home to 10 percent of the world's biodiversity, the country's beauty ranges over savannas, deserts, rain forests and mountains, and along the Pacific and Atlantic coasts. Colombia brings to mind emeralds, gold, colonial cities, culture, coffee, and the magical realms of Gabriel García Márquez.

A middle-income country at the end of the century, Colombia had benefited from six decades of steady GDP growth. The returns were significant: The poverty rate declined to 19 percent. Life expectancy rose to 69 years, and the infant mortality rate was slashed to 27 per thousand live births. Nevertheless, 30 percent of the rural population remained extremely poor, as did many city dwellers.

STRENGTHENED DEMOCRACY JUXTAPOSED AGAINST CONFLICT, VIOLENCE, AND DRUGS

Colombia has an active civil society and democratic institutions that have been expanding since the mid-eighties. In a process of decentralization, mayors have been locally elected since 1988 and governors since 1991. The Constitution of 1991 expands human rights, strengthens the judiciary, and enhances government accountability. It makes participation of citizens and nonprofit organizations a legal

Riot police (left) catch fire from Molotov bombs thrown by students in Bogota, September 1, 1999. The students were supporting a strike by public sector workers who were protesting policies they contended have impoverished them. Poverty exacerbates the problems resulting from the drug war, natural disasters, and environmental degradation. A boy carries a little firewood (above).

Overview

COUNTRY ASSISTANCE STRATEGY, 1998-2000

S trategy that sets the priorities for the Bank's assistance to the country; based on broad input from the top government leaders and representatives of civil society.

Bank Group contribution: Approximately US$1.6 billion during FY1998-2000

External partners: InterAmerican Development Bank, International Monetary Fund, Japanese Grant Fund, Global Environment Fund, Canadian Trust Funds, Andean Development Corporation

GOALS

Promote peace and development.

Promote rural development.

Attain public-sector responsiveness and efficiency.

Develop human capital.

Improve infrastructure services.

Ensure sustainable development.

COLOMBIA AT A GLANCE

Population: 40.8 million

Land area: 1,039,000 sq km

GNP: US$106.1 billion

GNP per capita: US$2,600

Poverty: 18% (of population below national poverty line)

Urban population: 74% of total population

Life expectancy at birth: 70 years

Infant mortality: 24 per 1,000 live births

Child malnutrition: 8% (of children under 5)

Access to safe water: 75% (of total population)

Illiteracy: 9% (of population age 15 and older)

With a list in hand, they entered the billiard parlour, Puerto Amor, and the soda shop, El Pariso, where they ordered those within to line up against the wall and proceeded to execute 11 people...

— *Internet report on 1999 human rights violations in the Magdalena Medio, from the Colombia Support Network*

right and, by creating new instruments, such as the plebiscite and the referendum, provides clear avenues for participation. It is hoped that these changes will eventually lead to a stronger civil society.

But Colombia may be better known for its violence than for its democracy. During the 1990s, the previously remote political violence spread, with various areas of the country subject to active disputes between guerrilla and right wing armed groups. Street crime, robbery, local drug trafficking, assault, and spouse and child abuse increased. One-quarter of all deaths were by homicide. It can be said without exaggeration that violence has come to dominate the daily lives of almost everyone.

A survivor (above) observes the wreckage of a small village in Cordoba State, 285 miles northwest of Bogota. The village was allegedly destroyed by rebels of the Revolutionary Armed Forces of Colombia in December 1998. At least 11 people were killed, and hundreds fled during clashes between guerrillas and rival paramilitaries. The village lies in a region of rich farmland, where rebels and the landowner-backed militias have battled for years. The region is also a corridor for illegal arms trafficking from Central America and the Caribbean.

In 1997, the World Bank Group and the Colombian government carried out one of their periodic planning exercises to set the priorities for the Bank's assistance to the country. Both the Bank and the government were keen on using a participatory approach, and the possibilities created by the new constitution provided an opening.

The participatory approach entailed workshops for the country team, the top government leaders, and representatives of civil society. In the workshops, the participants prioritized the country's development challenges and advised the Bank on its portfolio.

Then, the Bank and government blended the input, constructed an action plan, and formulated their agreement about the Bank's Country Assistance Strategy (CAS).

The government and citizen representatives successfully argued that violence had become the chief obstacle to development and should be the prime target for the CAS.

Political, economic, and social violence in Colombia have overlapping dimensions. In rural areas, for instance, unequal access to land and jobs raises the propensity for violence. The resulting general insecurity reduces the incentive to invest in agriculture and perpetuates the poverty and the violence.

A team from Colombia and the Bank reviewed the wealth of Colombian initiatives against violence. On a small scale, many had been effective. The team believed that such initiatives might have real impact if made part of a nationwide program. The team recommended a strategy with three building blocks:

NATIONAL LEVEL: incentives for peace, demobilization and reintegration of ex-combatants, reconstruction measures, and assistance to displaced persons—to accompany, and continue beyond, the peace negotiations.

SECTOR LEVEL: integration of violence-reduction efforts into education, judicial reform, job creation, and other diverse programs.

MUNICIPAL AND REGIONAL LEVEL: Small-scale grass-roots projects to rebuild trust and social cohesion.

If they bring us fairness instead of fumigation, find us decent prices for our fruit and beets, and begin building roads to get us to market, in six months, we will rip these flowers out ourselves.... If not, we will grow them as long as there's demand. And nothing can really stop us.

— *heroin grower in Turquestan, Huila, quoted by Alan Weisman, "The Cocaine Conundrum,"* Los Angeles Times, *September 24, 1995*

The participants in the planning process recognized the Bank's strengths in technical assistance and its access to worldwide knowledge, as well as the continuity the Bank can provide during local political change. They acknowledged the Bank's value in facilitating institutional change and its expertise in medium-term planning. They also noted that the Bank had become more client-oriented. But when invited to make drawings about their relationship to date with the Bank, they didn't mince words, or shall we say, pictures?

Sketched by participants in the national planning process, this drawing of the Bank's traditional diagnostic phase needs no translation.

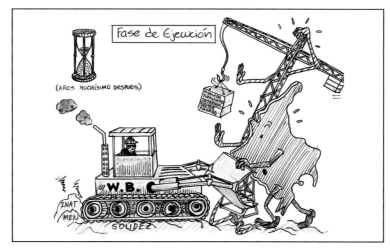

Execution phase: After years of complex processing, the Bank bulldozer goes into action. In the drawing, Colombia wishes it could be rescued by the private international financial market.

The cartoons were pretty funny; and we thought it was time to have a good laugh at ourselves. We have worked hard to improve the relationship, and we believe that the planning process helped.
— Jairo Arboleda, World Bank social development and civil society specialist

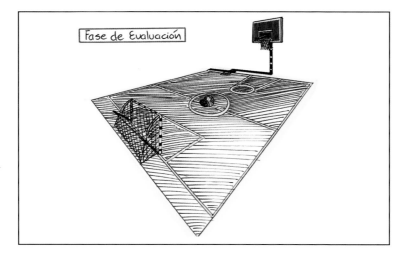

At evaluation time, the Bank and the Colombians find they each have been playing a different game.

Magdalena Medio is so bad that I have been able to visit only once, and security there has deteriorated since that visit. Our team feels an enormous responsibility to contribute the best we are capable of, as we know the leadership and staff of the consortium and the community members are risking their lives every day to realize their vision of a peaceful region where all the citizens can lead productive and fulfilling lives.
— Elsie Garfield, project task manager

To pay for the high costs of peace, the study recommends a systematic approach to taxes, peace bonds, and external assistance. These recommendations form the basis for many of the Bank-supported initiatives. For example, low-income youth are more likely than other groups to be both perpetrators and victims of crime. A youth development project aims to improve this group's life chances by building self-esteem, empowerment, and skills.

MAGDALENA MEDIO PROJECT

Situated in the heart of Colombia, Magdalena Medio is one of the poorest and most violent sections of the country. The area is a microcosm, containing all the actors and issues of Colombia's armed conflict—with guerrillas, right-wing "paramilitaries," and the army battling for control—while 70 percent of the population (500,000 people) lives below the poverty line.

Running any project in such an environment poses a daunting challenge. Facilitated by a consortium of the Catholic Church and an a nongovernmental organization, the Magdalena Medio Project aims to pave the way for a long-term program to reduce poverty and violence. The project is laying the groundwork by building

Nurturing, skill building, and fun can give a new life to the most discouraged child. The youngsters (below left) living in the desperately poor and violent Magdalena Medio area, have been organized to help clean up a polluted estuary so that it can again offer a livelihood to local fishermen. Their school provides related environmental studies. Working together can improve both infrastructure and community solidarity. Opposite, clockwise from top right: The hard work is completed, and the village inaugurates its new community center. Alternatives to coca cultivation and violence: cultural revival, saleable products, the communal pleasures of a regional fair.

and testing community approaches to development under conditions of extreme violence. These approaches include supporting
community-defined and managed projects in education, health,
environment, and economic development; seeking to revive long-
absent or weak community justice and municipal government;
strengthening the capacity of a voluntary citizens' network to
influence public affairs and develop local projects; creating education programs for peaceful coexistence and citizen participation;
and increasing jobs and income-generating opportunities for the
poor, particularly in rural areas.

The project has been supported by a US$5 million Learning and
Innovation Loan from the Bank plus US$1.25 million from the state
oil company.

With the support of the World Bank, the government is expanding the Magdalena Medio concept to other parts of the country and
is also establishing Peasant Enterprise Zones to offer alternatives to
coca cultivation.

Other Bank projects are also testing community approaches to
development in conflict areas. The hope is that by strengthening
communities and alleviating poverty through efforts chosen and led
by the citizens themselves, Colombia's democratic forces can gain
an advantage in their race against time.

The balance between people and nature is in jeopardy. Colombia has 10 percent of the world's flora and fauna and 19 percent of its bird species. It is rich in agricultural land, water, energy, and minerals. But one-third of Colombia's forests is already gone, and much of the nation's fragile beauty lies in areas subject to intense violence. Colombia has global priority for conservation. The Bank is supporting the government's decentralization of environmental management and integrated approaches to environment, development, and peace. In addition, it is supporting biodiversity conservation. Other traditional Bank projects continue with support for such sectors as education, water, sanitation, and roads. Technical assistance is part of the mix—for example, improved budget and tax administration and redistribution of land to the poor and family farmers.

At the turn of the century, democratic Colombia was gasping for life. Taking office in August 1998, President Andres Pastrana was faced with the continuing fallout from the Asia crisis: drastically lower coffee and oil prices, a deep recession, and the virtual shut-down of international credit markets to Colombia and other developing economies.

In the midst of a very difficult peace initiative, the new administration had to resort to deficit spending to cope with a sharp loss in tax revenues and shore up the ailing economy.

In 1999, the situation grew worse. In January, an earthquake struck the coffee region, killing 1,500 people and leaving 150,000 homeless.

The recession continued. GDP growth dove to a negative 4.5 percent in 1999, and it was the poor who suffered most. While the nearly 7 percent of the top fifth of the population lost their jobs, among the poorest fifth, unemployment reached 25 percent. Several million were left without health insurance. With youth unemployment

Earthquake compounds the problems. The earthquake of January 25, 1999 damaged 60,000 homes and disrupted power, water, and natural gas lines. The Bank responded with an emergency loan and redirected $93 million from other projects to help Colombia rebuild.

What will the World Bank do if the violence in Colombia increases further and the peace process goes nowhere? We are working in a country of heartbreak. We can only hope that we are helping Colombia find its way back from the brink to a new era of peace and development.
— Connie Luff, World Bank Colombia country officer.

reaching 44 percent, 150,000 students dropped out of secondary school.

Under the circumstances, the World Bank Group mobilized credits that had not been planned in the Country Assistance Strategy. The loans are badly needed to help cushion the impact of the recession on the poor, help rebuild the area devastated by the earthquake, and strengthen the banking system. With its modest external debt, Bank officials believed that Colombia could service the new loans.

With help from both the World Bank and the InterAmerican Development Bank, Colombia determined to expand its social safety net to about 3 percent of GDP. The programs include job training for 60,000 youth, 10,000 day care centers, more school lunches, community kitchens, and public works. In addition, the government will provide water and sanitation, temporary housing, and health services to about half a million people displaced by the armed conflict.

Efforts to improve health and education continued, with the goal of universal coverage.

PROJECT TEAM

Ernesto May and David Yuravlivker, task managers. Issam Abousleiman*, Jairo Arboleda*, Harold Bedoya, Susana Buenaventura, Karim Burneo*, Sandra Cardozo, Margarita Caro, Maria Elena Castro*, Krishna Challa, Eleo Codato, Connie Corbett, Ernesto Cuadra, Roberto Cucullu*, Mauricio Cuellar*, Elsie Garfield*, Natalia Gomez*, James Hanna, Cornelis de Haan*, Maria Teresa de Henao, Andres Jaime, Howard Jones,* Maritta Koch Weser, Martha Laverde*, Marco Mantovanelli, Patricio Marquez, Eugene McCarthy, Dan Morrow, Carmen Nielsen*, Marina Niforos, Joveida Nobakht, Fred Nunes, Jonathan Parker, Thakoor Persaud, Jayme Porto Carreiro, Joel Reyes, Anders Rudqvist*, Kathy Scalzulli, Miriam Schneidman, Julian Schweitzer, Teresa Serra. Paul Isenman and Andres Solimano, country directors. Felipe Saez*, resident representative. (*Core team for the Magdalena Medio project.*)

Vietnam

A STEEP CLIMB FROM STAGNATION TO PROSPERITY

In the 1970s, the independent and reunified Vietnam was determined to manage its economic affairs through central planning. This policy impeded recovery from 35 years of civil war, and the country stagnated. In the late 1980s, to revitalize its economy, Vietnam undertook a bold series of reforms, called "doi moi" (renovation). State collectives were gradually disbanded and people were allowed to work their own plots, start businesses, and seek wage-paying jobs. Price and interest rate controls were eased. Foreign trade and investment began to be liberalized. Private initiative was again encouraged, and the country set out to rebuild its legal system.

These reforms made Vietnam one of the fastest growing economies in the world. Income per head grew at more than 5 percent a year. From 1993 to 1998, the proportion of people in poverty fell from almost 60 percent to less than 40 percent. Agricultural production doubled, and Vietnam became the world's second largest exporter of rice.

In 1993, with the Cold War over, the stage was set for the World Bank to begin supporting Vietnam. From 1994 to 1998, the Bank Group's International Development Agency lent Vietnam US$2 billion at very long maturities and zero interest rates. More than half of these loans went to rehabilitate badly needed infrastructure while the rest went for agriculture and primary education.

With World Bank Group support, Vietnam is focusing more deeply on poverty, social issues, environment, and rural development.

If you love this vast hazy

world

Please come and build

the rice fields of

Vietnam with me.

The fields of my

homeland have turned

lush and green

And my heart opens like

a flower.

—Pham Duy, Vietnamese poet

Overview

COUNTRY ASSISTANCE STRATEGY, 1998-2002

World Bank Group strategy for its investments in Vietnam, based on the government's priorities and developed jointly through broad consultation with civil society and other major international assistance organizations.

GOALS

With poverty alleviation at the center, the Bank Group's Country Assistance Strategy (CAS) for Vietnam is designed around the government's program:

Improve macroeconomic stability and competitiveness; strengthen the financial sector; reform state-owned businesses; build roads, bridges, water systems, and other badly needed infrastructure; accelerate and diversify rural growth and increase environmental protection; invest in people and promote social equity; and improve public administration, transparency, and participation.

VIETNAM AT A GLANCE

Population: 76.5 million

Land area: 325,000 sq km

GNP: US$25.6 billion

GNP per capita: US$330

Poverty: 37% (percent of population below national poverty line)

Urban population: 24% (of total population)

Life expectancy at birth: 68 years

Infant mortality: 35 per 1,000 live births

Child malnutrition: 45% (of children under 5)

Access to safe water: 38% (of total population)

Illiteracy: 17% (of population age 15 and older)

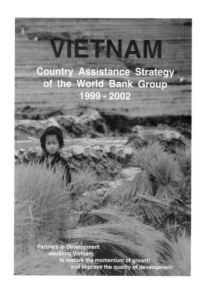

Partners that listen. The World Bank Group periodically conducts a planning process with each country in which it works. The 1998–2002 Vietnam Country Assistance Strategy (CAS) provides an example of the Bank's increasing emphasis on obtaining input from both government and civil society.

The Bank Group and the government held extensive consultations with officials, the ruling Communist Party, and the National Assembly. The domestic and foreign private sector; women's, farmers', and youth cadres; research institutes, nonprofit organizations, and multilateral and bilateral donors were drawn in as well. An important insight from the consultations was that the public was concerned about the quality of development, and not just the quantity.

IN THE LATE NINETIES, THE TAKEOFF FALTERS

The early reforms had freed the individual energies of the Vietnamese, thus leading to a vibrant informal sector. But big businesses were still owned and inefficiently operated by the state. The bulk of domestic savings was directed to investments in them. Medium- and small-scale private companies had yet to emerge, and the financial system remained weak.

The East Asia crisis slammed into the Vietnamese economy just as it was becoming clear that the first wave of reforms had reached their limits. By late 1990s, the Vietnamese economy was showing the strain.

Income disparities between city and countryside had increased. The growing informal sector, short of credit and lacking institutional support, could not generate enough jobs for the many young people entering the labor market every year. And past years of high growth, combined with weak enforcement of environmental policies, were threatening the country's natural resources. Both the momentum and the quality of Vietnam's development were in peril.

RESTORING MOMENTUM: NEW REFORMS AND THE 1998 COUNTRY ASSISTANCE STRATEGY

The economic slowdown led the government to rethink and consult broadly, internally as well as externally. The consultations, conducted in partnership with the World Bank Group, focused on restoring the momentum of growth and deepening the quality and sustainability of development. The new viewpoint is reflected in the 1998–2002 Country Assistance Strategy (CAS).

With poverty alleviation at the center, the CAS is designed around the government's seven-fold program: (1) improving macroeconomic stability and competitiveness; (2) strengthening the financial sector; (3) reforming state-owned businesses; (4) building roads, bridges, water systems, and other badly needed infrastructure; (5) accelerating and diversifying rural growth and increasing environmental protection; (6) investing in people and promoting social equity; and (7) improving public administration, transparency, and participation.

Veronique Danforth, manager of the World Bank book store (Info Shop) in Washington, D.C., has been invited to help set up a center that will offer information on all aspects of development in Vietnam. The center will include a video learning center, an open-stack library, a reading room, computers with Internet access, and a bookstore. Danforth has vividly registered the changes that have taken place in little more than a decade. "The timid opening toward free-market enterprise has released incredible productive capacity. You can see it everywhere. One woman squats on the curb with her sewing machine, repairing clothes for passersby. Another has a scale—for 3 cents you can be weighed. And even more carry huge loads, yoked and balanced across their shoulders, selling anything they can."

In parts of the North, there are many paths and almost no cars. Only a few people have bullocks and mules or beat-up old bikes. The rest just have their feet. They need better tracks so they can get to market to sell what they grow and buy what they need.
— *Thach Ngoc Phan, transport operations officer*

Ket Village (top left) grows enough rice for only three months. No agricultural extension worker has ever visited here. The land close to the houses could be used for irrigated paddy. There is a good water source only one kilometer away. The villagers identified irrigation as the top priority for assistance. The Bank is funding a community-based rural infrastructure project, in which communities can decide what local infrastructure improvements should be made.

The northern uplands (opposite) feature steep hills and no roads. This is a difficult physical environment with differing cultures and few natural resources. The Country Assistance Strategy lays out a new poverty reduction project to help the people in this region.

Education and human development. *It takes highly motivated students and teachers to do lessons knee-deep in water after a flood (far right). A Bank-supported education project will help improve the schools.*

In Vietnam, the desire for education is strong, and there is widespread recognition of its importance. But, in many schools, there is nothing on the walls, not even an alphabet. Many children have no books and simply copy what their teachers write on the blackboard. The Country Assistance Strategy aims to help the government target support for poor households and communities, to relieve their education costs and to improve the learning of their children. — *Mai Thi Thanh, education operations officer*

The CAS has two great strengths: It follows Vietnam's own priorities, and it is based on a broad consultative process, which engaged all key segments of society and the donors. We avoided a situation in which "one is going to live with a wife or husband who was arranged by one's parents but not by oneself" [Vietnamese saying]. For these reasons, the CAS has support among all of the partners.
— Naoko Ishii, country program coordinator

ENVIRONMENT. *The natural resource base of Vietnam, a very densely populated country, is seriously degraded. The Country Assistance Strategy aims to help protect natural resources and to ensure that people's livelihoods can continue to flourish.*

Three-quarters of Vietnam are hilly and mountainous. A third of the population lives in upland areas. This photo illustrates a common problem in the uplands: damage resulting from a combination of logging and clearing for cultivation. Vietnam has recently taken steps to begin controlling the logging industry, but a serious challenge remains: to create productive livelihoods for poor rural communities.
— Pham Hung Cuong
Rural Development Operations Officer

The key to reducing poverty and stimulating rural incomes is helping to create nonfarming jobs. We are therefore giving priority to policies and programs that encourage the development of small- and medium-sized enterprises. Our policy is to provide the poor with a fishing rod instead of fish.
— H.E. Mr. Tran Xuan Gia, minister for planning and investment.

COTTAGE INDUSTRIES: WELDING AND LOGGING. *State-owned enterprises have commanded the bulk of national bank financing. Regulations have not sufficiently considered the needs of middle-sized and small companies. This is gradually changing.*

With its nonconvertible currency and absence of a stock market, Vietnam was sheltered from the worst of the initial impact of the East Asia financial crisis. Unfortunately, while the other crisis-affected countries in the region responded with impressive structural reforms, Vietnam did not initially seize the opportunity to accelerate reforms. What Vietnam now urgently needs is to restore its attractiveness in international markets and ensure that every single dollar is spent with as much impact as possible. The slowdown of the late nineties must not be allowed to undermine the impressive progress in reducing poverty over the past decade. The government of Vietnam is aware of this and has committed itself to reenergize and deepen its "doi moi" process.
— Andrew Steer, country director

The Country Assistance Strategy supports a new generation of investments in poverty reduction. We will monitor results and feed them back into future design. Depending on changes in policy, portfolio performance, and impact on poverty, the Bank Group's assistance will range from US$300 to more than US$800 million a year.
— *Nisha Agrawal, principal economist and coordinator, poverty reduction*

CAS TEAM

Nisha Agrawal, principal economist and coordinator-poverty reduction. Jitendra N. Bajpai, Wolfgang Bertelsmeier, Philippe Fernand Boyer, Tosca Bruno-Van Vijfeiken, Tim Campbell, Choeng Hoy Chung, John Clark, William H. Cuddihy, Quynh Nga Dang, Tom Davenport, Alegria De La Cruz, Quen Do Duong, Carlos Escudero, Mario Fischel, Clifford Garstang, Kristalina Georgieva, Cong The Giang, Jeffrey Gutman, Donna Haldane, Dieter Havlicek, Althea L. Hill, Thanh Ha Hoang, Farrukh Iqbal, Naoko Ishii, Victoria Kwakwa, Alain L. Labeau, Ranjit Lambech, Morgan Landy, Minh Thi Nguyet Le, Jacques Loubert, Lars Lund, Thanh Thi Mai, Anil K. Malhotra, Kazi Mahub-Al Matin, Darayes Bahudur Mehta, Richard L. Meyers, Peter Russell Moock, Russel Muir, Quynh Hoa Ngo, Hoai Linh Nguyen, Khanh Nguyen, Ngan Thuy Nguyen, Nguyet Nga Nguyen, Phuong-Thao Nguyen, Than Xuan Nguyen, Thang Chien Nguyen, Thanh Cong Nguyen, Thuy Anh Nguyen, Van Linh Nguyen, Van Minh Nguyen, Kyle Peters, Cuong Hung Pham, Duc Minh Pham, Thack Ngoc Phan, Hoang Anh Phung, Pam Prangkham, Andrew Proctor, Shane Rosenthal, Louise Scura, Rebecca Sekse, Chris Shaw, Susan Shen, Jerry Silverman, Anil Sinha, Robb Smith, Paul Stott, Herawaty Sutrisna, Chris Thomas, Thang-Long Ton, Kim Thi Tran, Phuong Thi Lan Tran, Hung Tien Van, Somit Varma, Kimberly Versak, Phuong Anh Vu Tran, Huong Thu Vu, Leila Webster, Mei Xie, Wael Zakout. Andrew D. Steer, country director.

Bolivia

A NEW RECIPE FOR ATTACKING POVERTY

With mountains higher than 20,000 feet, a huge plateau at almost 12,000 feet, rain forests, a vast desert, swamps, and savannas, Bolivia is beautifully dramatic. The size of France and Spain combined, it is also sparsely inhabited, with somewhat under 8 million people. In the 1980s, the Bolivian economy was typified by its inflation rate: an unbelievable 24,000 percent. In the early 1990s, thanks to structural adjustment and financial reforms, the country brought inflation down to less than 4 percent in 1998 and went from economic decline to a healthy growth rate.

GROWTH WITHOUT POVERTY IMPACT

Despite being a leader in market reforms, Bolivia remains one of the poorest countries in Latin America. Its people are still suffering from decades of slow growth, limited investment in human capital, social segmentation and high inequality, and weak institutions.

The Bolivian Gross Domestic Product (GDP) is around US$1,000 per capita. About two-thirds of Bolivians are poor, with low levels of education, health, and nutrition. Ten percent of the children under

For a long time, the Bolivian development menu was limited to structural adjustment and financial stabilization. Now, the country is looking for a better diet. After consulting with his most loyal customers, the people, "Chef" Banzer, the President of Bolivia, asked the World Bank for advice on the best ingredients for poverty alleviation, growth, and strong institutions. In this cartoon from the Bolivian press, he is using the ingredients to make flan (pudding) just the way the Bolivians like it.

174

Overview

The Bolivian National Action Plan, formulated during 1997, grew out of a national dialogue sponsored by the Bolivian government and supported by the World Bank. The dialogue was developed by commissions representing the country's civil society. The international assistance agencies helping Bolivia also participated. The pillars of the strategy constitute the framework for the country's development program and for the World Bank Group's Country Assistance Strategy.

THE FOUR MAIN PILLARS OF THE STRATEGY

OPPORTUNITY: To generate higher economic growth with better distribution.

EQUITY: To raise standards of living of the poor.

INSTITUTIONALITY: To strengthen the institutional framework for better justice and a corruption-free administration.

DIGNITY: To remove Bolivia from the drug circuit by 2002.

See Appendix 11 for details.

CORE MEASURES OF SUCCESS

COUNTRY PERFORMANCE BENCHMARKS	1997	2000	2002
Poverty headcount ratio (%)	67.0	63.0	59.0
Poverty gap ratio (%)	32.0	29.0	26.0
Percent of children under five suffering malnutrition	10.0	8.5	6.0
Infant mortality rate, per 1000 live births	69.0	63.0	57.0
Maternal mortality rate, per 100,000 live births	390.0	340.0	290.0

BOLIVIA AT A GLANCE

Population: 7.9 million

Land area: 1,084,000 sq km

GNP: US$7.9 billion

GNP per capita: US$1,000

Poverty: 67% (of population below national poverty line)

Urban population: 63% of total population

Life expectancy at birth: 62 years

Infant mortality: 67 per 1,000 live births

Child malnutrition: 9% (of children under 5)

Access to safe water: 60% (of total population)

Illiteracy: 17% (of population age 15 and older)

The younger generation of Bolivia (left) will reap the fruits of the across-the-board reforms under way at the turn of the millennium.

five are malnourished. The average schooling is seven years. "After 10 years of external aid, totaling 7 percent of Gross Domestic Product," says Isabel Guerrero, World Bank country director for Bolivia, "Bolivia achieved macroeconomic stabilization. But there was no impact on poverty." But the Bolivians are committed to changing this. The focus of the current government's five-year effort (1997 to 2002) is poverty alleviation.

THE MIXING BOWL: THE COUNTRY ASSISTANCE STRATEGY

For every country it serves, the World Bank periodically prepares a strategic plan for its programs. Called the Country Assistance Strategy (CAS), this plan serves as the driving instrument for the Bank Group's partnership with the country and for managing resources in response to the country's priorities.

Reflecting the government's National Action Plan, the Bank's CAS for 1998–2002 aims to help the country to continue growth and to share the benefits broadly in the society. Its duration roughly coincides with term of Bolivia's president, Hugo Banzer. The Bank Group's International Finance Corporation participated in planning the CAS, which incorporates a private-sector strategy for Bolivia.

Country performance benchmarks, such as those in the CAS, are an indication that a government is serious about results. Such benchmarks, however, are a relatively new instrument in public administration. Development organizations and governments moving toward results-based management are struggling to make use of them. They are complicated to define, entail agreement among many players, and require monitoring and information systems that in many cases do not exist. What benchmarks are meaningful? How do you link an outcome indicator with meaningful output and input indicators? How do you divide responsibility for outcomes among the various partners? You can go crazy! But, although challenging,

I believe this is an effort with huge potential rewards. So far, our answers to these questions are not ideal, but they are good enough to begin with. What is important is to keep the focus on results, and learn by doing.
—Ernesto May, World Bank lead economist for Bolivia

Using a participatory approach, the Country Assistance Strategy
was prepared during late 1997 and early 1998.

The Bank team acted as partner and facilitator throughout. The
team and the authorities worked together to define the strategic
objectives for the Bolivians' plan; structure the consultative
approach; and rank the priorities for the Bank's development
lending.

The planning was conducted in phases:

National Dialogue—Representatives of civil society, October 1997.
Bolivia's development challenges and how to meet them. The con-
clusions form the basis for the five-year National Action Plan. (This
dialogue has been criticized for inadequate representation by NGOs
and the private sector. The Bank and the government have worked
since then to broaden inclusion in national poverty planning.)

Bank Group Country Team Workshop, November 1997. How to
support the Bolivians' strategies.

Joint Government/Bank Group Workshop, November 1997. Discussion of the National Action Plan and the corresponding Bank assistance strategy.

Joint Government-Donor Workshop, November 1997. Coordination of assistance to support the Bolivian program.

Consultative Group Meetings, April 1998. (For Bolivia, as for most
countries, the international donors and banks providing assistance
meet yearly to coordinate their policies, programs, and actions.)
Agreement regarding the external assistance program, as well as
monitoring and evaluation process.

CHANGING THE MIX OF SUPPORT

The Country Assistance Strategy called for the Bank to lend Bolivia
between US$200 million and $450 million during the period FY
1999–2002. The International Finance Corporation's plan for the
same period called for an additional $200 million in investments.

DEAR WORLD BANK, WE INVITE YOU
NOT TO COME. *In preparing the
country plan, the Bolivians were
eager to be in the driver's seat. They
asked the Bank team to stay in the
background. "With the national
dialogue," says Ernesto May, World
Bank lead economist for Bolivia, "the
Bolivians started a process where civil
society has a direct role in identifying
the counry's most important development priorities and suggesting what
actions should be taken. The government listened to the World Bank's
advice about how to structure the dialogue but it asked us not to attend.
The Bolivians want to make their
own decisions."*

*Participating in the National
Dialogue, October 1997, La Paz.
Campesino shakes hands with the
vice president of Bolivia (left).*

The Bolivians laid out how they wanted the Bank Group to support the government's strategies:

OPPORTUNITY: Building roads, establishing a regulatory framework, and supporting financial services [Multilateral Investment Guarantee Agency (MIGA) and IFC] in order to achieve the GDP growth necessary for poverty reduction. (GDP, or Gross Domestic Product is the total goods and services produced by a country.)

EQUITY: Supporting infrastructure and services for the poor and socially excluded and reinforcing the participatory methods that Bolivia has pioneered. These enable the government to be more responsive to the needs of the poor.

INSTITUTIONALITY: Completely overhauling public sector management, including the civil service, the judiciary, and the budget system—all necessary to focus on results, tackle corruption, and improve governability.

The Bolivians also indicated that they were satisfied with the contributions of other organizations in the areas of environment and micro-credit, so the Bank has backed away from any new projects in these fields.

THE COMPREHENSIVE DEVELOPMENT FRAMEWORK

The Bolivian exercise in developing this Country Assistance Strategy was one of 14 experiments using the World Bank's Comprehensive Development Framework (the CDF). The CDF is a tool to help lay out multiple priorities and clarify government, donor, and creditor responsibilities. The idea is to harmonize what Bank Group President James D. Wolfensohn calls "two parts of a duet, . . . [the] macroeconomic on the one side and the social, structural, and human on the other." (For details see appendix II, page 193–195.)

This harmonization can bring social programs and policies powerfully into play in tackling poverty.

TOUGH ACCOUNTABILITY STANDARDS

The government, the World Bank Group, and the international donors assisting Bolivia will measure themselves by tough standards. By defining country performance benchmarks, the Country Assistance Strategy ensures that the government and its partners stay focused on results. (See *Core Measures of Success* in overview on page 176.)

A village plans and builds a water and irrigation project. The villagers themselves (above) do a great deal of the work.

With the support of the World Bank Group and other international assistance organizations, Bolivia has chosen to tackle a considerable list of priorities. Among them is rural development. In the past, agricultural policies and institutions have tended to favor the wealthy commercial large-scale farmers rather than poor small farmers. The new strategy gives emphasis to helping rural communities, indigenous people's organizations, small farmers' associations and women's groups to design and implement their own initiatives. These groups are choosing such projects as access roads, irrigation, agricultural processing, and natural resource management.

When you think about it, the nurturing of children is fundamental for the future of the country. Prior to the age of six, the most rapid mental and social development takes place. The children in the day care center (opposite) may look middle class but, in reality, they are extremely poor. Most of them live in the humblest of homes. The centers are clean and safe places to learn and grow. Impact evaluations show a significant effect on the psychosocial development and nutritional status of the children who attend. The centers mean that mothers can work and earn money. By the end of December 1999, with World Bank support, the government had furbished and rehabilitated more than 2,800 such centers.
—Deborah Bateman, World Bank Group resident representative in Bolivia

Cutting palmetto in the Chapare region (right). Eighty percent of the rural population of Bolivia perceives that their income level has stagnated or dropped during the 1990s, according to a recent rural productivity study. The Country Assistance Strategy aims to reverse this.

In 1998 Bolivia's GDP grew at almost 5 percent, but fell almost to a halt in 1999 due to the adverse effects of El Niño and the Asian crisis.

Reforms and decentralization proceeded. In fact, Bolivia's strong track record and progress toward social development made it the second country in the world and the first in Latin America to qualify for debt relief under the Bank's HIPC (Heavily Indebted Poor Countries) initiative. The Bank's US$450 million in debt relief allowed Bolivia to increase spending in the social sectors, which accounted for 50 percent of the 1999 budget.

Very low taxes and poor tax collection are behind the fiscal deficits of many developing countries. In the past, Bolivia was no exception. But in the nineties, the government has made strides in revenue collection, from well below 10 percent of GDP in the mid-1980s to more than 20 percent in 1999. In the near future, a switch from a complicated value added tax to a simple personal income tax is expected to further improve tax collection. Much of the revenue is being directed to the local level, where citizens are being trained and organized to participate, maintain oversight, and insist on accountability.

In the past, Bolivian governance has been greatly impeded by corruption. The Bolivians are determined to put an end to the cheating. In 1998, the government established a 10-year National Integrity Program. A major component of the program has been public-sector modernization. In 1999, the Bolivian Congress passed landmark civil service reforms, including performance incentives. Timeliness and accuracy of public-sector financial accounting reduce the opportunities for corruption. A Bank credit is supporting the institutional reform effort.

An independent judiciary is also indispensable in the fight against corruption. The Bolivians recently took an important step by reforming the selection of the Supreme Court and other judges. The Bank is supporting judicial training.

Underscoring its commitment to cleaning up, in 1999 the Bolivian government placed several Supreme Court judges and other senior government officials under investigation. Officials are also required now to declare their assets, and the audit capacity of the comptroller general is being improved.

Down the line, could a different administration reverse the commitment to results-oriented management and accountability? What about public unrest if expectations for improvement are not met quickly enough? Indeed, early in 2000, violent demonstrations were mounted in La Paz and Cochabamba to protest proposed water fee hikes and slow economic growth, and the Banzer Administration imposed a two-week state of siege.

"There is always a possibility that the reforms could be brought to a halt," says Ernesto May. "But the expanding involvement of all development participants—civil society, political parties, external agencies, and the private sector—in the national integrity drive gives us great hope."

Deborah Bateman (above) the Bank Group's resident representative in Bolivia, visits a day care center in La Paz, part of the Intergrated Child Development Project, sponsored by the World Bank.

COUNTRY PLANNING EVOLVES

The World Bank's approach to country planning has continued to evolve. At the end of 1999, the World Bank and the International Monetary Fund introduced a new, joint planning process. The two institutions said, "The aim . . . will be to strengthen country owner-ship of Poverty Reduction Strategies, improve coordination among development partners and, perhaps most important, focus the ana-lytical, advisory, and financial resources of the international com-munity on achieving results in reducing poverty."

The process will resemble that of the Comprehensive Develop-ment Framework, seeking to balance social needs with financial and macroeconomic policies. (See appendix 11, page 193.)

The World Bank and the IMF agreed in 1999 to require that nations seeking subsidized lending or debt relief under the Heavily Indebted Poor Countries Initiative (HIPC) prepare PRSPs. This will enable Bolivia to benefit from a second round of HIPC, following another national dialogue in spring 2000.

CAS TEAM

Ernesto May, team leader. Jose Alonso-Biarge. Oscar Alvarado, Patricia Alvarez Chris Barham, Debbie Bateman, William Battaile, Paul Beckerman, Juan Cariaga, Maria Elena Castro, Daniel Cotlear, Willem Floor, Sue Goldmark, Norman Hicks, Olympia Icochea, Evangeline Javier, Chakib Khelil, Toshiya Masuoka, Mat McMahon, Caroline Moser, Inés Mosquera, Deepa Narayan, Hoveida Noback, Alberto Nogales, Fred Nuñez, Izumi Ohono, Luis Pisari, Cesar Plaza, Luis Ramirez, Gary Reid, Carlos Reyes, Salvador Rivera, Edgard Rodriguez, Sandra Rosenhouse, Enrique Rueda, Bernard Sheahan, Jyoti Shukla, Maurice Sterns, David Tuchschneider, Pietro Veglio, Eloy Vidal, Hermann Von Gersdorff, Michael Walton, Pierre Werbrouck. Isabel Guerrero, country director.

Bolivia provides a clear example of the fact that economic stabilization and market reforms are not enough for poverty reduction. After 10 years of external aid, totaling 7 percent of Gross Domestic Product, there has been virtually no impact on poverty. As the century turns, it is very satis-fying for the World Bank Group team to work hand-in-hand with the Bolivians on their new and much-needed commitment to the poor.
— *Isabel Guerrero, Bolivia Country Director*

President Banzer's customers (left) helped to make Bolivia's flan. Of course, the proof of the pudding will be in the eating.

In April, 2000 violent protests erupted in Cochabamba and other parts of Bolivia. The protesters were objecting to a proposed hike in Cochabamba's water charges and expressing discontent about slow economic growth. The government responded by reshuffling the cabinet and appointing a commission to look for solutions to Cochabamba's water situation.

In May, 2000, the government began a new National Dialogue, consulting at the municipal and national levels, to re-tool the country's poverty reduction plans.

Evaluating Impact

One of the purposes of this volume is to recognize the importance of systematic monitoring and evaluation (M&E) of the poverty reduction impacts of development interventions. The activities depicted here offer good practice examples of M&E. The stories were selected by a team representing the World Bank's Poverty Reduction Board, the External Affairs Department, and the Bank Group's Staff Association. Completed projects had to demonstrate an impact on poverty, and ongoing projects had to incorporate promising evaluation components. The charts in this appendix summarize such information for most of the projects described in the book. Kalanidhi Subbarao, lead economist, and Gloria Martha Rubio Soto, research analyst, of the World Bank poverty anchor, provided the comments at the bottom of each chart.

Some definitions may be helpful. Every project or program intervention with inputs of various kinds leads to tangible, physical *outputs* (e.g., kilometers of road or number of schools built or potable drinking water facilities provided). *Monitoring* is the continuous assessment of project implementation. It provides program managers and other stakeholders with information about input use and corresponding output generation, identifies potential problems, and facilitates timely adjustments in the project's operational details.

The term *outcomes* refers to the direct effect of outputs on individuals or households. An example is the enrollment rate following the construction of a school. *Impact evaluation* consists of assessing outcomes and, thus, the medium or long-term developmental results. Impact evaluation provides program administrators and policy makers with an understanding of the observable effects (both intended and unintended) of an intervention on individuals or households. Evaluation helps in determining what does or does not work in a given setting. It provides a basis for the modification of current activities and the design of future interventions. Impact evaluation helps maintain accountability for public funds.

Good data are a prerequisite for sound evaluation. Information about socioeconomic characteristics of program participants and nonparticipants is essential for impact evaluation. To measure outcomes most reliably, this information should ideally be collected before and after the project on the *same* participant and nonparticipant households (panel data sets), the latter serving as control groups. Where panel data sets are unavailable, techniques exist that can help disentangle the net impact of interventions from other nonproject influences. In all circumstances, it is highly desirable to *integrate quantitative and participatory methods* into the evaluations.

Development organizations have not always incorporated sound evaluation practices into their work. However, M&E is now recognized as a very important tool in the development process. The World Bank and other international development agencies have increasingly required that monitoring and evaluation be a component of their activities. It is hoped that this book will help further this commitment.

Country: ARGENTINA

Project name: MATERNAL AND CHILD HEALTH AND
NUTRITION PROJECT I AND II (PROMIN)

INDICATORS AND TARGETS

The indicators and targets for this project are (1) reduce the proportion of underweight babies to 7 percent; (2) reduce the proportion of malnourished pregnant women by 30 percent; (3) reduce the proportion of malnourished children from birth to age five by 50 percent; (4) increase the proportion of women receiving maternal and prenatal care to 60 percent; (5) increase to 60 percent the proportion of children from birth to age six receiving health care; (6) increase the proportion of children fully vaccinated to 80 percent; and (7) improve clients' perceptions of access to, use of, and satisfaction with health care services.

METHODOLOGY

Regular anthropometric and socioeconomic surveys will be conducted in the target communities by volunteer women, assisted by health personnel. Survey data will be supplemented with data on birth weights from hospital statistics.

Coverage of services will be measured regularly through the Health Management Information System.

PARTICIPATORY EVALUATION

Beneficiary assessments are conducted regularly to collect information on client satisfaction and use of services.

COMMENTS

The evaluation component could be strengthened by specifying an appropriate counterfactual situation and collecting the necessary information to isolate the net impact of the project.

Country: ARGENTINA

Project name: SECOND SOCIAL PROJECT
(TRABAJAR II PROGRAM)

INDICATORS AND ACHIEVEMENTS

From May 1997 to November 1999, 650,000 temporary jobs were created. The gross income per month per worker over about five months was US$200 on average. Eighty percent of the workers were from the poorest 20 percent of Argentine households, with more than half from the bottom 10 percent.

METHODOLOGY

The most commonly used methods to estimate household income without intervention were not feasible in the case of the TRABAJAR program: No randomization had taken place to construct a control group to which to compare the income of project beneficiaries; and no baseline survey was available, ruling out the possibility of conducting a before-and-after evaluation. Thus, the evaluation technique adopted consisted in comparing the income of participants with that of "similar" nonparticipants, identified ex-post using a propensity-score matching method based on a number of observed characteristics. Specifically, a comparison group was constructed by matching program participants to eligible nonparticipants from the population over a set of socioeconomic variables such as schooling, gender, housing, subjective perceptions of welfare, and membership in political parties and neighborhood associations.

DATA SOURCES

Two household surveys were used to evaluate this program. One is a national socioeconomic survey, Encuesta de Desarrollo Social, from which the comparison group was constructed. The second data set is a special purpose sample of project participants. Both surveys were conducted using the same questionnaire and the same interviewing teams, and both were conducted at approximately the same time.

COMMENTS ON EVALUATION ACTIVITIES

This project is a good example of how an impact evaluation can be conducted even when no baseline data are available and no provisions were made at the beginning of the project for constructing a control group.

Although a qualitative approach was followed during the survey questionnaire design, the evaluation could have been further strengthened by also including a participatory evaluation of the process that yielded the project outcomes. In fact, in the follow-up project, some qualitative research was carried out among groups of workers and the agencies sponsoring projects. This work supplemented previous qualitative research, which had been done as part of the social assessment that examined issues related to the participation of NGOs and women in the program.

Country: BANGLADESH
Project name: FEMALE SECONDARY SCHOOL ASSISTANCE PROJECT

INDICATOR, BASELINE, TARGET, AND ACHIEVEMENT

From a 1993 baseline of 238,000 girls enrolled in grades six to ten (the early grades of secondary schools in Bangladesh), the target was to increase girls' enrollments to 516,000 by 1999. In actuality, the project surpassed its target: By 1998, 861,000 girls were enrolled.

BASELINE

Data were collected from Bangladesh educational statistics, population census, and household expenditure surveys.

Studies on parents' attitudes, financing of secondary education, and occupational skills, as well as special school profile surveys, were conducted in the project areas.

FOLLOW-UP DATA

The project's MIS system tracks key student and school indicators such as enrollment, attendance, performance, promotion, student-teacher ratios, stipend and tuition payments, and other selected indicators for all project components.

CONTROL GROUPS

Use of control groups was planned but, due to a nationwide expansion of the program, control groups were not set up.

PARTICIPATORY EVALUATION

During the project mid-term review, several rapid studies were conducted. Beneficiary assessments among parents, students, and teachers were carried out to assess enrollment, performance, dropout rates, attractiveness of stipends, school attendance, and management of the stipend program.

COMMENTS

Although a thorough evaluation has not been done, relevant information for impact evaluation has been collected. One could try to distinguish the net effect of the project on enrollment rates using the available information and conducting an econometric analysis. Additional beneficiary assessments can be done at the end of the project to complement the mid-term evaluation.

Studies are planned to assess the impact on fertility, health, and children's education of a pilot female secondary education program financed by NORAD. Other studies will assess the increase of women in the labor market, especially in the teaching profession. These studies may also help to better understand the impact of this Bank intervention.

Country: BENIN
Project name: COMMUNITY-BASED FOOD SECURITY PROJECT

INDICATORS, TARGETS, AND ACHIEVEMENTS

This project originally was scheduled to end in 1999, but it was extended to 2000. The most recent comprehensive studies to determine impact took place in 1997; the figures listed here cover the 1998 targets and project achievements by the end of 1997: (1) With a target of 300 new income-generating microprojects in the project area, the number actually achieved was 1,412. (2) With a target of 32,500 direct beneficiaries, the actual achievement was 31,905. (3) With a target of 30,000 children under growth and health status surveillance, the project actually brought 18,000 children under surveillance. (4) With a target of 7,500 pregnant and 7,500 lactating women under close supervision, the project actually brought 800 pregnant women and 4,500 lactating women under surveillance. (5) With a target of a 24 percent reduction in malnutrition (from a level of 35 percent), the project achieved an estimated 17 percent reduction. The lower achievements in several categories were due to delays in the beginning of the project.

BASELINE

During the project's pilot phase, socioeconomic and anthropometric surveys covered 869 households in 11 sub-districts.

As part of the mid-term review, a qualitative assessment of the project was conducted. A sample of 56 groups of beneficiaries were selected from target sub-districts where NGO capacity has been strongest and where only minimal delays were experienced in delivering project support.

Results from qualitative assessments helped identify areas in which the project was having a positive impact as well as areas that required special attention.

FOLLOW-UP SURVEYS

The National University of Benin managed collection data from household surveys and NGO monitoring reports from a sample of 56 groups of beneficiaries.

CONTROL GROUP

Matching methods will be used to construct a control group.

COMMENTS

This project presents a sound plan for impact evaluation. It also shows the advantages of using participatory evaluation techniques during project implementation to introduce needed mid-course corrections in project design.

Country: EL SALVADOR
Project name: SECONDARY EDUCATION PROJECT

INDICATORS, BASELINE, AND TARGETS

For this project the indicators, baseline, and 2002 targets are as follows: (1) From a 1997 baseline of 18 percent, increase the gross enrollment rate of public upper secondary students to 23 percent. (2) From a 1997 baseline of 78 percent, increase the transition rates between 9th and 10th grades to 90 percent. (3) Significantly increase the mean achievement scores for mathematics, language, and science tests. Baseline and targets are being developed.

BASELINE

A household survey was conducted in 1996, during the preparation phase of the project. This survey provided initial data on household socio-demographic characteristics, level of education of family members, attitudes towards schooling, and reasons for not attending school.

A national assessment system (NAS) has been established in the Ministry of Education (MINED) to monitor the quality of secondary education. All graduating secondary students are required to take a national student achievement test (PAES). In addition, the NAS has begun to apply achievement tests in mathematics, language, and science to a random sample of 9th grade students. These tests will provide baseline data for future assessments.

FOLLOW-UP DATA

MINED is upgrading an information system to provide better statistical data on education indicators and continual assessment of the of the national education program.

The NAS will continue to administer the PAES to all graduating secondary students on an annual basis, as well as the achievement tests to a random sample. In addition, information on contextual variables will be collected from directors, teachers, students and school councils.

CONTROL GROUPS

No control groups were set up because all secondary schools in El Salvador are covered under this national program.

PARTICIPATORY EVALUATION

Beneficiary assessments will be conducted throughout the life of the project to measure progress and guide future actions. These evaluations will include the various institutions that have been contracted to provide services to MINED.

Results from the quantitative assessment and participatory evaluation will be triangulated to obtain a better understanding of the impact of the project.

COMMENTS

Control or comparison groups may be constructed even in national interventions if program services are to be phased in. In any case, the analysis should ensure that the net effect of the project is properly isolated from that of external factors.

This project is a good example of how to combine quantitative and qualitative participatory approaches for evaluating project impacts.

Country: INDIA

Project name: UTTAR PRADESH SODIC LANDS RECLAMATION PROJECT

INDICATORS	BASELINE 1993	ACHIEVEMENTS TO DATE	TARGETS END PROJECT (2001)
Number of hectares reclaimed	—	47,677 ha	69,000 ha
Number of poor families benefited	—	85,000	175,000
Cropping intensity			
B class land (single cropped)	80%	200%	At least 200% for all
C class land (no crop)	0	200%	At least 200% for all
Annual average family income (Rs./family/year)	Rs.12,000	Rs.20,000	—
Internal rice and wheat availability (grams/person/day)	220 gr./ 240 gr.	610 gr./ 660 gr.	—
Number of women's self-help groups formed (WSHGS)	—	2,019	3,000
Savings by WSHGS	—	Rs.8.6 million	—

ENVIRONMENTAL IMPACT			
Soil quality	Sodic	Improved physical properties	Expansion of productive lands
Ground water quality change	Good	No negative impact	Maintain the quality
Biodiversity	Poor	Improved habitat for insects, small mammals, and birds	Increase the biodiversity

BASELINE

Socioeconomic survey of a 10 percent sample of project beneficiaries to collect data on household characteristics, landholding, agricultural production, and migration.

Geographic Information System and associated database.

Aerial photos taken at the beginning of the project.

Regular soil sampling and ground water testing.

Biodiversity studies to establish the situation of plant, insect, small mammal, and bird populations before reclamation.

FOLLOW-UP SURVEYS

Socioeconomic surveys conducted annually.

Changes in spectral patterns using IRS LISS-2 images to be collected, covering each area at the time of reclamation and five and eleven years later.

Aerial photos taken at the end of the project.

Regular soil sampling and ground water testing.

Biodiversity studies during the year of reclamation and five and eleven years thereafter. Information is collected on the lands of people who are also the subjects of the socioeconomic evaluation, so that correlations can be made.

CONTROL GROUP

The project's socioeconomic impact is assessed by using reflexive controls (before and after situation).

The environmental impact is assessed by using control plots outside the immediate project areas.

PARTICIPATORY EVALUATION

Beneficiary assessments are conducted annually.

COMMENTS

This complex project has many objectives and outcomes but provides for a reasonably good impact evaluation of both environmental and socioeconomic outcomes.

The evaluation could have been strengthened further by ensuring the integrity of the control groups through selecting control plots that are not exposed in any way to the benefits of the project. The integrity of control groups drawn from right outside the project areas may be compromised if project benefits, such as the influence of link drains, spill over on to neighboring plots.

Country: INDIA
Project name: FIRST TAMIL NADU INTEGRATED NUTRITION PROJECT (TINP)

INDICATORS, TARGETS, AND ACCOMPLISHMENTS: 1982–90

For this project, the target was to reduce by 50 percent (from a level of 60 percent) severe and moderate malnutrition among children six to 36 months old. The actual achievements were a 26–42 percent reduction in severe malnutrition in different project areas and a 14–21 percent reduction in the number of children below 75 percent of median weight-for-age. Reduction in moderate malnutrition proved more difficult. A second target was to reduce the infant mortality rate by 25 percent (from a level of 125 per 1,000). The actual achievements were a 26–29 percent reduction in earlier phases of the project and a 12-13 percent reduction in the later phases.

BASELINE

Data were collected from a stratified random sample of 1,100 Community Nutrition Centers (CNCs) in 11 districts in 1982 (the start of the project in several districts). The data cover all children ever enrolled in the selected CNCs and include monthly weights of each child, as well as service delivery and use indicators and socioeconomic data.

FOLLOW-UP SURVEYS

Data from the sample of CNCs collected in 1986 and 1990.

CONTROL GROUP

Data from the National Nutrition Monitoring Bureau were used to compare declines in malnutrition between districts covered by the project and districts not covered.

Multivariate analysis was used to distinguished the effect of the TINP from other concurrent nutrition programs.

COMMENTS

The evaluation, conducted by the Bank's Operations Evaluation Department (OED), is a good attempt to isolate the net effect of the Tamil Nadu Integrated Nutrition Project from other confounding factors. However, the evaluation was not able to clarify to what extent the declines in infant mortality rates can be attributed exclusively to the project.

A lesson is that more concrete steps needed to be taken at the beginning of the project for incorporating all elements of evaluation, including participatory evaluation.

Country: MADAGASCAR
Project name: COMMUNITY NUTRITION PROJECT

INDICATORS, BASELINE, AND TARGETS

Indicators, 1998–99 baseline data, and 2003 targets for this project: (1) From a baseline of 45 percent (national average) of children under three years, reduce chronic malnutrition (stunting) in children under three by 30 percent. (2) With data collection in progress to establish a baseline, reduce Vitamin A deficiency in children under three by 30 percent. (3) Improve community awareness of malnutrition and capacity to take action. Knowledge, attitude, and practice studies are in progress.

BASELINE AND FOLLOW-UP DATA

Planned or completed surveys:

Anthropometric: 1998 (baseline), 2000, and 2003.

Vitamin A prevalence: 1998 (baseline) and 2003.

Iron deficiency: 1998 (baseline), 2000, and 2003.

Helminth infections prevalence: 1998 (baseline), 2000, and 2003.

Dietary behavior: 1998 (baseline), 2000, and 2003.

Consultants will conduct before-and-after analyses of indicators to assess the impact of the project.

Beneficiary assessments will be conducted during the project to assess changes in the knowledge, attitudes, and practices of project beneficiaries.

Substantial efforts have been made to collect relevant data for impact assessment. However, concrete plans for evaluation are still to be defined. Timely incorporation of evaluation activities into project design provides the opportunity to select the most appropriate methodology. This is critical in nutrition interventions because projects are usually in the regions with the highest malnutrition, thus introducing a placement bias that needs to be corrected to assess the true impact of the interventions.

Country: MALI
Project name: GRASS-ROOTS INITIATIVES TO FIGHT HUNGER AND POVERTY

Beneficiary communities will identify indicators of project success from their perspective during the initial participatory survey. These indicators will be augmented by others defined by key partners.

Local NGOs or consulting firms will conduct participatory community surveys in each targeted village.

Survey of knowledge, attitudes, and practices will be conducted by NGOs or consulting firms in communities selected using a purposive sampling methodology

The monitoring and evaluation system will collect information on the indicators identified by the communities. The project management office will analyze these data and measure perceived improvements in living standards and decision-making capacity.

To measure behavioral changes that the project may have engendered, follow-up surveys of knowledge, attitudes, and practices will be conducted.

Not available yet but can be constructed by collecting household data and using matching methods.

This project takes an innovative participatory approach for impact evaluation that fully involves project stakeholders, especially villagers.

The evaluation component could be improved further if the existing qualitative methods were supplemented with a quantitative, structured, survey-based evaluation.

Country: MOROCCO
Project name: RURAL ROADS PROJECT

Off-farm employment as measured by the number of days worked outside the farm increased by six times from 1985 to 1995. In control areas, the number of days tripled. Primary school enrollment rates more than doubled from 28 percent in 1985 to 68 percent in 1995.

In control areas, these enrollments increased to a level of 51 percent in 1995. Frequency of visits to health centers increased from 2.8 days per year before the project to 5.6 days per year after the project. Such visits in control areas increased from 3.7 days per year to 5 days per year.

The impact evaluation study compares changes in outcome and impact indicators before and after the intervention between project and comparison roads. Four out of ten rural roads paved under the Bank's project were included in the study. They were selected to maximize diversity in agro-climatic conditions, economic characteristics of the zones, and economic function of the roads. For each project road, a nearby road that had not been subject to improvement during the study period was selected as a comparison road. Although no baseline data had been collected, changes before and after the project were measured using information from retrospective questions.

Socioeconomic data from project and control roads were collected through several surveys at the household, village, and farm level.

Focus-group interviews were conducted in each of the villages included in the study. This information complemented the survey data and provided additional insights in the development process of the project.

COMMENTS

One of the lessons from this evaluation is the importance of early incorporation of sound impact evaluation activities into the project cycle. Although an intention to collect baseline information existed at the start of the project, in practice no data were collected. Moreover, control roads selected during project appraisal had to be changed for the ex post evaluation because the roads in the initial group had been improved or had become different from project roads. Two main efforts were made to correct these deficiencies: First, retrospective information was collected at the end of the project; and second, new comparison roads were selected. This evaluation illustrates how lost ground can be retrieved and informed judgment be derived on the impact of the project.

Country: PERU
Project name: SIERRA NATURAL RESOURCES MANAGEMENT AND POVERTY ALLEVIATION PROJECT

INDICATORS AND TARGETS

The project indicators and 2001 targets for the project area are (1) increase production in selected micro-catchment areas by 25 percent; (2) cultivate 90 percent of the rehabilitated areas; (3) place 25 percent of the area under agroforestry protection; (4) raise the number of producers using improved seeds to 25 percent; (5) benefit 75,000 families; and (6) attain the participation of 20 percent of the women.

BASELINE

Community data from 66 micro-catchments (44 project participants and 22 nonparticipants) were collected by the project preparation team using participatory techniques

FOLLOW-UP AND OTHER SURVEYS

Data from the same communities included in the baseline will be collected and analyzed by an NGO hired by the Ministry of Women and Human Development three years after the project start. Quantitative data on project participants from the MIS will also be used for impact evaluation.

CONTROL GROUP

Baseline and follow-up community surveys contain information on both project participants and nonparticipants (control group).

COMMENTS

Participatory evaluation includes information on both project participants and nonparticipants to assess the counterfactual situation. Evaluation activities can be further strengthened by complementing the participatory evaluation with a quantitative evaluation also aimed at assessing the counterfactual situation. In the absence of a baseline survey, matching methods seem to have some potential for a quantitative evaluation.

Country: PHILIPPINES
Project name: LGU URBAN WATER AND SANITATION PROJECT

INDICATORS, BASELINE, AND TARGETS

For this project, the indicators, 98 baseline, and 2007 targets are as follows: (1) Raise the percentage of target area residents receiving a reliable water supply at least 16 hours a day on a sustainable basis to 90 percent. (2) Increase the percentage of urban population with access to safe drinking water from 60 percent to 90 percent. (3) Increase the percentage of wastewater being collected and treated in the 20 largest cities outside Manila to 80 percent (no baseline number available).

BASELINE

Household surveys conducted during the preparation of feasibility studies will collect baseline information from participating and nonparticipating towns on several socioeconomic variables such as family size, income level, source of water supply, and sanitation.

FOLLOW-UP DATA

The project will commission a follow-up survey after the systems are fully operational to evaluate whether the intervention is generating the envisaged benefits. These data will be complemented with information from the project MIS and census data.

CONTROL GROUPS

Nonparticipating communities will be used as comparison groups.

Beneficiary assessments will be conducted as part of the first Adjustable Program Loan (APL). Lessons learned from these assessments will be considered to plan the participatory evaluation activities of the rest of the APL program.

INNOVATIVE FEATURES OF THE PROJECT

The project will provide water supply infrastructure on the basis of consumer demand. Consumers' wishes and their willingness to pay for services are being elicited before the engineering designs are finalized. Thus, the incentives between the seller and the buyer of water supplies are aligned. Buyers are willing to pay a higher price, provided the services meet their requirements (i.e. convenience, quality, reliability, etc.). Sellers are motivated by the profits to sell maximum water at the price. This represents a radical departure from prevailing Philippine water supply project practices in which the end users are never consulted systematically on either service levels or tariffs.

To ensure sustainability after the infrastructure has been completed, the project is facilitating the participation of professional private-sector operators. This will ensure that systems are operated and maintained sustainably. For the targeted class of municipal-managed systems, this is a significant innovation because it mitigates the risk of political interference preventing cost recovery and consequent deterioration in the constructed infrastructure. In the old style, the sellers were supposed to perform a social function but, in fact, had disincentives to serve consumers efficiently.

This is the first water supply project in the Bank using the APL instrument.

COMMENTS

US$500,000 has been allocated for monitoring and evaluation activities. It is hoped that local capacity for evaluation—which is quite high in the country—will be used for assessing program impacts, including sustainability of created infrastructure.

Country: UGANDA
Project name: NUTRITION AND EARLY CHILDHOOD DEVELOPMENT PROJECT

INDICATORS, BASELINE AND TARGETS

For this project the indicators, 1997 baseline, and 2003 targets in the project areas are as follows: (1) From a baseline of 25 percent, the project aims to reduce the percentage of underweight children under six to 16 percent. (2) The project aims to reduce dropout rates (baseline, 46 percent) and repetition rates (baseline, 15 percent) at the lower primary level to 36 percent and 10 percent respectively. (3) From a baseline of 44 percent, the project aims to reduce worm load (hookworm) in children to 22 percent. (4) From a baseline of 25 percent, the project aims to increase the number of mothers practicing appropriate child care to 50 percent.

BASELINE

Household surveys were conducted at the beginning of the project. These surveys included modules on household socio-demographic characteristics; knowledge, attitude, and child rearing practices of the principal caregivers; child health; anthropometric information and cognitive assessments of children under the age of six.

Community surveys were also conducted to gather information on local conditions common to all households in the area.

FOLLOW-UP SURVEYS

Household surveys covering the same sample will be conducted two years after the initial baseline survey by a private consulting firm hired by the project under the supervision of a World Bank Development Economics Research Group (DECRG) team and the Government Project Office. Results of the evaluation are expected in 2001.

CONTROL GROUP

The survey will cover a total of 2,250 households in 50 parishes randomly assigned to treatment and control groups.

PARTICIPATORY EVALUATION

Participatory evaluations will be conducted throughout the project cycle to assess progress in project implementation and to help guide future courses of action. These evaluations will use a purposive sampling method and will be contracted to a local consulting team.

COMMENTS

This project is an excellent example of sound impact evaluation design. It combines both quantitative and participatory approaches and provides the necessary elements to assess the net impact of the project.

One remarkable feature of this intervention is that the evaluation strategy was built into the design at the beginning of the project.

The Comprehensive Development Framework and the Poverty Reduction Strategy Paper

COMPREHENSIVE DEVELOPMENT FRAMEWORK

The Comprehensive Development Framework (CDF) approach calls for a development plan 'owned' by the country itself, focused on a long-term vision of the results to be achieved, and supported by strong partnerships among governments, donors, civil society, the private sector, and other development actors.

In launching the Comprehensive Development Framework, the Bank has focused attention on what it sees as the essential building blocks for effective development:

STRUCTURAL: good governance and clean government, an effective legal and judicial system, a well-organized and supervised financial system, and a social safety net and social programs.

PHYSICAL: water and sewerage, energy, roads, transport and telecommunications, and environmental and cultural issues.

SPECIFIC STRATEGIES: for rural, urban, and private sector development

Additionally, each country has its own unique priorities. Attention to macroeconomic and fiscal issues, trade and regulatory issues, the labor market and employment conditions, and the role of the private sector, for example, depends on the characteristics of the country and the results of the national dialogue about priorities and programs needed to address them.

POVERTY REDUCTION STRATEGIES

In late 1999, the World Bank and the International Monetary Fund (IMF) announced a joint Poverty Reduction Strategy initiative. This initiatives draws upon the Bank's experience with the Comprehensive Development Framework and reflects a growing convergence of views among national governments, the World Bank, the IMF, United Nations agencies, regional development banks, nongovernmental organizations, and church groups.

The focus of the Poverty Reduction Strategies is on identifying in a participatory manner the poverty reduction outcomes that a country wishes to achieve and the key public actions—policy changes, institutional reforms, programs, projects, and so on—that are needed.

The underlying principles are that Poverty Reduction Strategies should be country-driven, oriented to achieving concrete results, comprehensive in looking at cross-sectoral determinants of poverty outcomes, informed by a long-term perspective, and providing the context for action by various development partners.

Three steps underlie the development of Poverty Reduction Strategies: (1) Understanding the nature and locus of poverty—who the poor are, where they live, and their sources of livelihood. Poverty is multi-dimensional, extending from low levels of income and consumption to poor health, lack of education, gender disparities, powerlessness, and social exclusion. (2) Choosing public actions that have the highest poverty impact. (3) Selecting and tracking outcome indicators. The choice of indicators and their monitoring should be done transparently and in a participatory fashion so as to ensure that there is broad societal consensus on the impact of the strategy and that any changes needed are indeed implemented.

Poverty Reduction Strategies will form the basis for World Bank (International Development Agency) and IMF concessional assistance to low-income countries. Initial efforts will support the development of such strategies in countries expected to be eligible for debt relief from the Bank, the IMF, and other creditors under the HIPC (Heavily Indebted Poor Countries) initiative. At the same time, the new approach will be introduced in a phased manner in all low-income countries receiving concessional assistance from the World Bank and the IMF.

The above information is excerpted from the World Bank and IMF Web sites. See www.worldbank.org/poverty/strategies or www.imf.org for details.

The table, right, translates Bolivia's Country Assistance Strategy into the Bank Group's Comprehensive Development Framework. Across the top of the chart is a list of the four "pillars" of Bolivia's poverty alleviation plan. These pillars are based on the national dialogue carried out in the beginning of the Bolivian president's term (1997-2002). The left-hand side of the table shows some of the key development actors who can support the Bolivian government's plans for Bolivia. The small boxes identify key strategies and stakeholder responsibilities.

1998–2002 COMPREHENSIVE DEVELOPMENT FRAMEWORK FOR BOLIVIA: POVERTY ALLEVIATION

OPPORTUNITY

Higher Rates of Sustainable Economic Growth

	Infrastructure	Regulatory Framework for PSP	Financial System	Natural Resources and Environment
World Bank Group	Transport: Rural Infrastructure Rural Water and Sanitation Municipal Development El Niño IFC Water in La Paz MIGA power and infrastructure guarantees	Regulatory Reform Privatization	Financial Regulatory Reform MIGA Services for Investing in Banking IFC financial Inst. for microfirms	Biodiversity Conservation Environment Industry and Mining
IDB	Transport: Power Urban Development Housing	Water Regulatory Reform Sectoral Privatization	Environmental Regulations	Ecological Tourism
Other Donors	CAF Roads Korea Roads	Canada Private Investment Development Sweden Industrial Cooperation	USAID Micro-finance CAF Financial System Expansion	USAID Natural Resources KFW Biodiversity UNDP Ecological Tourism and Biodiversity
Private Sector	Telecomm Water Power		Banks Insurance Co.	
NGOs	Local NGOs		Local NGOs	Local NGOs

194

	EQUITY			INSTITUTIONALITY			DIGNITY		
Improve Income Distribution and Inclusion				*Governability for Opportunity and Equity*			*Remove Itself from the Coca Drug Trafficking Circuit*		
Rural Development	**Income and Productivity of the Poor and Indigenous**	**Social Services for Gender and Excluded Groups**	**Decentralization and Community Empowerment**	**Efficient and Transparent State**	**Judicial Reform**	**Corruption**	**Alternative Development for Coca Areas**	**Coca Crops Eradication**	**Enforcement Policy**
Agro Technology Rural Communities Development Land Administration	Participatory Rural Investment Indigenous Peoples Social Investment Fund	Education Quality Education Reform Health Sector Child Development Secondary and Higher Education	Municipal Development Financial Decentralization	Institutional Reform Public Expenditure Review Decentralization and Accountability	Judicial Reform National Integrity	National Integrity			
Agricultural Sector	Basic Sanitation for Small Municipalities Micro-enterprise	Education Reform Basic Health Child Development	Strengthening Social Participation	National Governance	Justice Program				
Netherlands Rural Telecoms. and Energy Spain Rural Power UNDP Information Capacity NDF Land Administration Denmark	OPEP Rural Water and Sanitation KFW sewerage Denmark and FIDA Indigenous	Sweden and UNDP Education Reform Germany Education Quality UNICEF Health, Nutrition and Sanitation UNDP and USAID Health	Netherlands Administrative Decentralization UNICEF and EU Municipality Strengthening	USAID Governance Sweden, Denmark and GTZ Civil Service		Complementary activities by USAID and GTZ	USAID Alternative Development UNDCP Alternative Development	USAID Eradication UNDCP	
Local NGOs	Local NGOs	Local NGOs	Local NGOs						USAID

195

The World Bank Group

The world's largest source of development assistance, the World Bank provides nearly US$30 billion in loans annually to its client countries. The Bank uses its financial resources, its trained staff, and its knowledge base to help each developing country onto a path of stable, sustainable, and equitable growth. The main focus is on helping the poorest people and the poorest countries.

The World Bank is owned by more than 180 member countries whose views and interests are represented by a Board of Governors and a Washington-based Board of Directors.

Founded in 1944, the World Bank today consists of five closely associated institutions:

IBRD: THE INTERNATIONAL BANK FOR RECONSTRUCTION AND DEVELOPMENT

The IBRD, which accounts for about three-fourths of the Bank's annual lending, provides loans and development assistance to middle-income countries and creditworthy poorer countries.

IDA: THE INTERNATIONAL DEVELOPMENT ASSOCIATION

IDA, established in 1960, is focused on the poorest countries. IDA credits account for about one-fourth of all Bank lending. Borrowers pay a fee of less than 1 percent of the loan to cover administrative costs. Repayment is required in 35 or 40 years with a 10-year grace period. Nearly 40 countries contribute to IDA's funding.

IFC: THE INTERNATIONAL FINANCE CORPORATION

IFC promotes growth in the developing world by financing private sector investments and providing technical assistance and advice in partnership with private investors.

MIGA: THE MULTILATERAL INVESTMENT GUARANTEE AGENCY

MIGA helps encourage foreign investment in developing countries by providing guarantees to foreign investors against loss caused by non-commercial risks.

ICSID: THE INTERNATIONAL CENTRE FOR SETTLEMENT OF INVESTMENT DISPUTES

ICSID provides facilities for the settlement—by conciliation or arbitration—of investment disputes between foreign investors and their host countries.

Source: This information comes from the Web site: www.worldbank.org

Abbreviations and Definitions

ABBREVIATIONS

APL: Adaptable Program Loan, World Bank

CAS: Country Assistance Strategy, World Bank

CDF: Comprehensive Development Framework, World Bank

DANIDA: Danish International Development Agency

GDP: Gross domestic product

GNP: Gross national product

HIPC: Heavily Indebted Poor Countries, international initiative

IBRD: International Bank for Reconstruction and Development, World Bank Group

IDA: International Development Agency, World Bank Group

IFC: International Finance Corporation, World Bank Group

IMF: International Monetary Fund

MIGA: Multilateral Investment Guarantee Agency

NGO: Nongovernmental organization

OED: Operations Evaluation Department, World Bank

PILSA: Community-based Food Security Project (Benin)

PREM: Poverty Reduction and Economic Management Network, World Bank

PROMIN: Health, Nutrition, and Early Childhood Development Project (Argentina)

PRONAMACHS: Sierra Natural Resources Management and Poverty Alleviation Project (Peru)

PRSP: Poverty Reduction Strategy Paper, World Bank and International Monetary Fund

SEECALINE: Surveillance et Éducation des Écoles et des Communautés en matière d'Alimentation et de Nutrition Élargie (Madagascar)

TINP: Tamil Integrated Nutrition Project (India)

UNICEF: United Nations Children's Fund

DEFINITIONS

Access to safe water. The percentage of the population with reasonable access to an adequate amount of safe water (including treated surface water and untreated but uncontaminated water, such as from springs, sanitary wells, and protected boreholes). In urban areas, the source may be a public fountain or standpipe located not more than 200 meters away. In rural areas, the definition implies that members of the household do not have to spend a disproportionate part of the day fetching water.

Child malnutrition (percent of children under 5). The percent of children under five years of age whose weight for age and height for age are less than minus two standard deviations from the median for the international reference population aged 0–59 months. The reference population, adopted by the World Health Organization in 1983, is based on children from the United States who are assumed to be well nourished.

Gross national product. The sum of gross value added by resident producers (plus taxes less subsidies) and net primary income from nonresident sources.

GNP per capita. GNP per capita is the gross national product divided by midyear population figures in U.S. dollars.

Illiteracy rate. The percentage of adults aged 15 and above who cannot, with understanding, read and write a short, simple statement about their everyday life.

Infant mortality rate. The number of infants who die before reaching one year of age, per 1,000 live births in the same year.

Life expectancy at birth. The number of years a newborn infant would live if prevailing patterns of mortality at the time of its birth were to stay the same throughout its life.

Poverty rate. The percentage of the population living below the national urban poverty line. Developing these figures and drawing comparisons within and between countries is problematic. To indicate such comparisons roughly, the figures presented here incorporate various statistical methods, such as purchasing power parity, which take into account the local prices of goods and services.

Note: These definitions are from the World Bank's *World Development Indicators,* 1999.

Bibliography

Much of the information used in this book came from internal project reports and reviews, interviews, e-mail, and correspondence. The country data in the overview sections of each chapter come from the World Bank's *World Development Indicators,* 1999. Sources of the chapter epigraphs are listed under Credits, page 205. The sources in this bibliography are publicly available. On the assumption that readers are likely to want to know more about some, but perhaps not all, of the places mentioned in the book, I have arranged the bibliography by geographic location, followed by sections on monitoring and evaluation and general references.

General information about the World Bank can be found on the Bank's Web site at http://www.worldbank.org

ARGENTINA

Aiyar, Swaminathan S.A. "Lessons in Designing Safety Nets." *PREM Notes,* no. 2, April 1998.

"Argentina's Mr. Boring Plods to Victory by Default." *The Economist,* 4 September 1999.

Cichero, Daniel; P. Feliu; and M. Mauro. "Argentina. Consultations with the Poor." Report for the World Bank Global Synthesis Workshop, September 22–23, 1999.

Faiola, Anthony. "Argentina's Lost World. Rush into the New Global Economy Leaves the Working Class Behind." *Washington Post,* 8 December 1999.

_____. "Argentines Turn Against Peronists." *Washington Post,* 26 October 1999.

_____. "Deep Recession Envelops Latin America." *Washington Post,* 5 August 1999.

_____. "First Class Health and Child Care in the Slums." *Washington Post,* 8 December 1999.

Hay, Andrew. "Casting a Clear Eye on the Dirty War." *Washington Post,* 9 September 1999.

Krauss, Clifford. "The Buck Doesn't Stop Here: Now Argentina May Adopt It." *New York Times,* 25 February 1999.

_____. "Downshifting in Argentina; Recession and Rivalries with Brazil Stall the Economy." *New York Times,* 5 August 1999.

Krugman, Paul. "Don't Laugh at Me, Argentina. Serious Lessons from a Silly Crisis." *www.slate.com* Archives, 19 July 1999.

World Bank. "World Bank Approves First-Ever Policy Based Guarantee for $US250 Million to Argentina." News release 2000/043-LC, 16 September 1999.

BANGLADESH

Bangladesh, Government of. "Female Secondary School Assistance Project." Ministry of Education, Directorate of Secondary and Higher Education, undated.

_____. *Stipend Operation Manual,* Ministry of Education, Directorate of Secondary and Higher Education. Final draft, January 1996.

Pfohl, Jacob. "The Female Secondary School Assistance Project (FSSAP) of Bangladesh." Paper for SA Casebook Project on Gender and Participation.

Rai, Lekha. "Bangladesh. Plans and Priorities." (Interview with Sheikh Hasina, Bangladesh prime minister) *Washington Post,* 26 March 1999.

World Bank. "Consultation with the Poor: Participatory Poverty Assessment in Bangladesh." Report for the World Bank Global Synthesis Workshop, September 22–23, 1999, and Poverty Group, PREM.

World Bank Group. "Bangladesh." Country brief, 1998.

_____. "Bangladesh: Meeting the Challenge of Poverty Alleviation." 1998.

_____. "Promoting Girls' Education in Bangladesh. Female Secondary Assistance Project." 1998.

_____. "Pioneering Support for Girls Secondary Education: The Bangladesh Female Secondary School Assistance Project, Draft Project Brief." Undated.

BOLIVIA: IFC

Young, John E. "Mining the Earth." Paper no. 109. Worldwatch Institute, Washington, D.C., 1992.

BOLIVIA: CAS

Krauss, Clifford. "Bolivia, at Risk of Some Unrest, Is Making Big Gains in Eradicating Coco." *New York Times,* 9 May 1999.

Wamey, Julius. "The Comprehensive Development Framework: A Compass, Not a Blueprint, for Development." *Bank's World,* 3, no. 8 (1999).

World Bank. "Bolivia: Consultations with the Poor." Report for the World Bank Global Synthesis Workshop, September 22–23, 1999.

_____. "World Bank and IMF Endorse Strengthening National Ownership of Poverty Reduction Strategies." News release 2000/163-S, 22 December 1999.

_____. "World Bank Finances Regulatory Reform in Bolivia." News release 99/2013-LAC, 19 November 1998.

COLOMBIA

Carrigan, Ana. "Colombia's Best Hope." *The Nation,* 19 August 1999.

"Controversia." *Segunda Etapa,* no 174 (Junio 1999).

Dehasse, Joelle. "Colombia's Campesinos Seek Peace and Empowerment." *Bank's World,* 4, no. 13 (1999).

Gaag, Jacques van der, and D. Winkler. "Children of the Poor in Latin America and the Caribbean." World Bank LASHC paper series 1, July 1996.

Márquez, Gabriel García. "The Solitude of Latin America." Nobel Prize Lecture, 8 Dec. 1982.

McGirk, Tim. "A Carpet of Cocaine." *Time,* 9 August 1999.

Schneidman, Miriam. "Targeting At-Risk Youth: Rationales, Approaches to Service Delivery and Monitoring and Evaluation Issues." World Bank LASHC paper series 2, July 1996.

Weisman, Alan. "The Cocaine Conundrum." *Los Angeles Times Magazine,* 24 September 1995.

World Bank. "Colombia: Economic and Social Development Issues for the Short and Medium Term" Report 18394-CO, 19 November 1998.

_____. "World Bank Approves $506 Million for Financial Sector Reform in Colombia." News release 2000/101-LAC, 18 November 1999.

_____. "World Bank to Contribute $1.4 Billion to Colombia Support Package." News release 2000/055-LAC, 27 September 1999.

EL SALVADOR

Dos Santos, Madalena. "Social Assessment and the El Salvador Basic Education Modernization Project." World Bank Environment Department Dissemination Notes no. 28, August 1995.

Granzow, Sandra. "El Salvador Rebuilds Schools from the Grassroots Up." *EDI Forum,* 1, no. 4 (1997).

Meza, Darlyn. "Decentralizacion Educativa, Organizacion y Manejo de las Escuelas a Nivel Local—El Caso de El Salvador: Educo." *Informe,* no. 9 (Mayo 1997).

Navarro, Mireya. "Salvador's Leader May Blend a Guru's Nonviolence with Right-Wing Politics." *New York Times,* 9 March 1999.

Pena, Valeria Junho. "Social Assessment: El Salvador Basic Education Modernization Project." World Bank LATEN dissemination note, no. 13, 1995.

Winkler, Donald. "Decentralizacion de la Educacion: Participacion en el Manejo de las Escuelas al Nivel Local." *Informe,* no. 8. (Mayo 1997).

World Bank. "World Bank Helps Finance Education Reform Project in El Salvador." News release 1775-LAC, 7 May 1998.

ESTONIA

International Finance Corporation. "Investment Assessment Report Non-Capital Markets Operation Portfolio Committee Edition. Estonia: Kunda Nordic Cement A/S," 13 November 1998.

Karmokolias, Yannis. "Cost Benefit Analysis of Private Sector Environmental Investments: A Case Study of the Kunda Cement Factory." (International Finance Corporation, Washington, D.C., Discussion Paper 30, undated.)

Noorkoiv, Rivo; P. F. Orazem; A. Puur; and M. Vodopivec. "How Estonia's Economic Transition Affected Employment and Wages (1989–95)." Policy research working paper 1837, 1997.

Swardson, Anne. "Six Nations Are Invited to Apply to Join EU." *Washington Post,* 11 December 1999.

INDIA: TAMIL NADU

Chaubey, Selina. *Catch Them Young.* Washington, D.C.: World Bank, 1998.

Measham, Anthony, and M. Chatterjee. *Wasting Away: The Crisis of Malnutrition in India.* Washington, D.C.: World Bank, 1999.

World Bank. OED 1994 Impact Evaluation Report.

_____. "Consultation with the Poor. India 1999: A Study Commissioned by Poverty Reduction and Economic Management Network of the World Bank to Inform World Development Report 2000–01." Report for the World Bank Global Synthesis Workshop, September 22–23, 1999.

_____. "Despite Health Improvements, Malnutrition Remains a Silent Emergency in India." News release 2000/087-SAR, 11 November 1999.

_____. "Tamil Nadu and Child Nutrition: A New Assessment." OED Precis 87, April 1995.

World Bank Group. "India." Country brief, 1998.

_____. "South Asia." Regional brief, 1997.

INDIA: SODIC LANDS

World Bank Group. "Sodic Lands Reclamation: Successful Participatory Management in Action." Project brief, 1998.

MADAGASCAR

Aubel, Judi. *Methodology for the Identification of PVO Child Survival "Best Practices."* Arlington, Va.: Basic Support for Institutionalizing Child Survival (BASICS), 1997.

Gottert, Peter. "Community Approaches in Madagascar." Paper presented September 17–19, 1997. Arlington, Va.: BASICS.

Helitzer-Allen, Deborah; and G. Newes Adeyi. "Program Guide for Planning Behavior Change Programs." Unpublished paper for BASICS, 23 January 1996.

Marek, Tonia. "Two Community Nutrition Projects in Africa. Interim Results." The World Bank, Washington, D.C., Findings, #112, June 1998.

Murray, John; G. Newes Adeyi; J. Graeff; R. Fields; M. Rasmuson; R. Salgado; and T. Sanghvi. *Emphasis Behaviors in Maternal and Child Health: Focusing on Caretaker Behaviors to Develop Maternal and Child Health Programs in Communities.* Arlington, Va.: BASICS, 1997.

MALI

Fusilli, Jim. "The Blues by Way of Mali." *Wall Street Journal,* 3 October 1999.

MOROCCO

Gentile-Blackwell, A. "From Foodline to Lifeline: Rural Roads in Morocco." World Bank OED Precis 119, June 1996.

"Morocco. Poised for Growth." *Washington Post,* advertising supplement, 14 December 1999.

Royaume du Maroc. Ministere des Travaux Publics. *Programme National de Construction de Routes Rurales,* Octobre 1996.

Trueheart, Charles. "Young King Pursues Own Vision for Morocco." *Washington Post,* 16 November 1999.

World Bank. "Morocco's Potential Still Unrealized." OED Precis 152, June l997.

PERU

World Bank. "World Bank, Peru, and Rural Communities to Finance Poverty Project in the Sierra Region of Peru." News release no. 97/1236-LAC, 16 January 1997.

PHILIPPINES

Moore, Debra; and L. Sklar. "Reforming the World Bank's Lending for Water: The Process and Outcome of Developing a Water Resources Management Policy," in *The Struggle for Accountability: The World Bank, NGO's and Grassroots Movements,* edited by Jonathan A. Fox and L. David Brown. Cambridge, Mass.: MIT Press, 1998.

Zanini, Gianni. *Philippines, from Crisis to Opportunity.* Washington, D.C.: World Bank Operations Evaluation Department, 1999.

UGANDA

Slater, Sharon; and C. Saade. *Mobilizing the Commercial Sector for Public Health Objectives.* Arlington, Va.: BASICS, 1996.

World Bank. "A New Partnership: Kampala Meeting Engages Government, Civil Society, and Donors." News release no. 99/2034/AFR, 10 December 1998.

World Bank. "Post-Conflict Reconstruction: Uganda. Case Study Summary." OED Precis 171, Summer 1998.

VIETNAM

Vietnam-Sweden Mountain Rural Development Programme, ActionAid, Save the Children Fund (UK) and Oxfam (GB). "Consultations with the Poor: A Synthesis of Participatory Poverty Assessments from Four Sites in Vietnam: Lao Cai, Ha Tinh, Tra Vinh & Ho Chi Minh City." Report for the World Bank Global Synthesis Workshop, September 22–23, 1999.

"Goodnight, Vietnam. Foreign Direct Investment." *The Economist,* 8 January 2000.

Keenan, Faith. "What's the Rush? Vietnam Reacts Slowly to Technology Wave." *Far Eastern Economic Review,* 15 July 1999.

Templer, Robert. *Behind the Bamboo Curtain. Shadows and Wind. A View of Modern Vietnam.* Boston: Little Brown, 1998.

Vatikiotis, Michael. "Behind the Bamboo Curtain. Interview—Books." *Far Eastern Economic Review,* 11 February 1999.

MONITORING AND EVALUATION

Baker, Judy L. *Evaluating the Poverty Impact of Projects: A Handbook for Practitioners.* Washington, D.C.: World Bank, 1999.

Ezemenari, Kene; A. Rudqvist; and K. Subbarao. "Impact Evaluation: A Note on Concepts and Methods." World Bank Conference on Evaluation and Poverty Reduction, June 14–15, 1999.

"Measuring Poverty at the Country Level." Full text at *http://www.worldbank.org/poverty/mission/up2.htm.*

Weaving, Rachel; and U. Thumm. "Evaluating Development Operations: Methods for Judging Outcomes and Impacts." *Lessons and Practices,* no. 10, November 1997.

World Bank. "Building Evaluation Capacity." Lessons and Practices, no. 4, November 1994.

_____. "Development Effectiveness, 1998: Opportunities in a Volatile Environment." OED Precis 175, Winter 1999.

GENERAL

Buckley, Robert. *1998 Annual Review of Development Effectiveness.* Washington, D.C.: World Bank, 1999.

Colletta, Nat J.; M. Kostner; and I. Wiederhofer. *The Transition from War to Peace in Sub-Saharan Africa.* Washington, D.C.: World Bank, 1996.

Demery, Lionel; and Michael Walton. *Are Poverty Reduction and Other 21st Century Social Goals Attainable?* Washington, D.C.: World Bank, 1998.

Ferreira, Francisco; G. Prennushi and M. Ravallion. "Macroeconomic Crises and Poverty: Transmission Mechanisms and Policy Responses." World Bank paper, 15 April 1999.

Haggard, Stephen; and S.B. Webb (eds.). *Voting for Reform: Democracy, Political Liberalization, and Economic Adjustment.* New York: Oxford University Press, 1994.

Hunger Project. *Ending Hunger: An Idea Whose Time Has Come.* New York: Praeger, 1985.

Lapierre, Dominique. *The City of Joy.* New York: Warner Books, 1985.

"Measuring Up for Aid." *The Economist,* 8 January 2000.

Narayan, Deepa. *The Contribution of People's Participation: Evidence from 121 Rural Water Supply Projects.* Washington, D.C.: World Bank, 1994.

_____. "Participatory Evaluation: Tools for Managing Change in Water and Sanitation." World Bank Technical paper 207, 1993.

_____, with Raj Patel, Kai Schafft, Anne Rademacher, and Sarah Koch-Schulte, *Voices of the Poor: Can Anyone Hear Us?* New York: Oxford University Press, 2000.

"New Corruption Indexes of Transparency International: Wide Range of Scores." *Transition, The Newsletter about Reforming Economies,* 10, no. 5, October 1999.

"Old Battle; New Strategy." *The Economist,* 8 January 2000.

Pearlstein, Steven. "Trade Theory Collides with Angry Reality." *Washington Post,* 3 December 1999.

Salmen, Lawrence E. *Listen to the People. Participant-Observer Evaluation of Development Projects.* New York: Oxford University Press, 1987.

Stiglitz, Joseph . "Launch of the 1999 World Development Indicators." Opening remarks for the release of the World Bank's World Development Indicators, 26 April 1999.

Swardson, Anne. "A Rorschach Test on Trade. Nations' Diverse Goals Color Reactions to Protests." *Washington Post,* 3 December 1999.

Wamey, Julius M. "Can Corruption be Measured? Bank Offers Diagnostic Tools to Measure and Combat Corruption in Member Countries." *Bank's World,* 4, no. 14, June 1999.

Wolfensohn, James D. "Coalition for Change." Address to the World Bank board of governors, 28 September 1999.

_____. "The Other Crisis." Address to the World Bank board of governors, 6 October 1998.

Wolfensohn, James; and Joseph Stiglitz. "Growth Is Not Enough." *Financial Times,* 22 September 1999.

World Bank. *Assessing Aid: What Works, What Doesn't, and Why.* New York: Oxford University Press, 1998.

_____. "Better Health for Africa." *Findings, Africa Region,* no. 46, November 1999.

_____. "Communication for Behavior Change." Workshop for task team leaders and human development staff, 4 March 1998.

_____. *The East Asian Miracle: Economic Growth and Public Policy.* New York: Oxford University Press, 1993.

_____. "Guinea: Moving Towards Food Security." *Findings, Africa Region,* no. 28, May 1998.

_____. "Latest World Bank Poverty Update Shows Urgent Need to Better Shield Poor in Crises." News release no. 99/2214-/s, 2 June 1999.

_____. "Lessons from Africa's Social Funds and Public Works and Employment Projects." *Findings,* no. 122, November 1998.

_____. *World Bank Participation Sourcebook.* Washington, D.C.: World Bank, 1996.

_____. "World Bank Review Shows Improved Project Performance, Underlines Importance of Strong Institutions." News release no. 99/2073-S, 21 January 1999.

_____. *World Development Indicators 1999.* Washington, D.C.: World Bank, 1999.

_____. *World Development Report 1999–2000: Entering the 21st Century.* Annual report, 1999.

Acknowledgments

This book has its origins in a revolving photo exhibition, illustrating the World Bank Group's work and mounted at World Bank headquarters during 1999.

Under the auspices of the World Bank Staff Group Staff Association, the Staff Association Poverty Working Group, and the Poverty Reduction and Economic Management unit of the Bank, the photo exhibit stories have been completely rewritten and updated for the book. The Bank's media devision sponsored the book's Web site, which is available through www.worldbank.org. A number of the Bank's senior managers funded the book and personally helped when the effort may have flagged. I owe them deepest thanks: James D. Wolfensohn, Sven Sandstrom, Peter Woicke, Shengman Zhang, Masood Ahmed, Kemal Dervis, Luis Descaire, Eduardo Doryan, Motomichi Ikawa, Motoo Kusakabe, Johanes Linn, Mieko Nishimizu, Callisto Madavo, Jean-Louis Sarbib, and Vinod Thomas. Margarita Bellinger, Jaime Carvajal, Andrew Ewing, Doug Forno, Paul Hubbard, Achim von Heynitz, Phil Karp, John Muir, and Tony Wan were also decisive and warm champions.

The book was shaped through consultation with and substantial contributions from the task managers, country directors, economists, country officers and team assistants listed in each chapter. They provided documents, correspondence, analytical and editorial input, and answers to many queries. To supplement their own photographs, they commissioned photography and escorted the photographers to remote corners of the featured countries. Two of these photographers, Marge V. Palmre and Abdeljalil Bounhar, conducted field interviews, which enriched the Estonia and Morocco stories. The chapter about India's Tamil Nadu Nutrition Project owes much to a monograph and photos by Selina Chaubey. The book belongs to all of these generous people and their partners in development.

I also appreciate the sustained and enthusiatic commitment of Jamil Sopher, former chair of the Staff Association, and the support of Thierry Brun and the Poverty Working Group. Without them, the book would not have found a home. Assuming the Staff Association chair in January, 2000, Morallina George added her support.

Gloria Martha Rubio Soto, research analyst, Kalanidhi Subbarao, lead economist of the World Bank's poverty anchor, and Michael Walton, director of the Bank's poverty reduction board, gave extensive time and gracious support. They provided a critical review of the projects proposed for selection and performed a cross-cutting role throughout. They were true partners. Indeed, the book would not have been possible without them.

Ms. Rubio and Mr. Subbarao also reviewed drafts of the manuscript, as did Lynne Sherburne Benz, senior economist; Iona Sebastian, former World Bank economist; and my husband, James M. Kearns. All brought a lifetime of working in development to their reading and gave insightful editorial input.

Njeri Kamau and Naye Bathily, while handling many endless details of preparing the book for publication, brought the kindest of friendship, belief, tact, and moral support. Marie-Claude Helman, Gladys Gicker, Alessandra Cortese, and Anu Oinas provided invaluable institutional and logistical assistance.

Paul O'Connell and Cynthia Casas, who represent the World Bank to Epcot and the World's Fair 2000 in Hanover, were equally generous. Thanks to them, three of the Bank's displays at the World's Fair are drawn from stories in the book. They helped work out the sale of the book in both locations.

Members of the Bank's media division, under the supervision of Caroline Anstey, extended themselves with enthusiasm and kindness. Nicole Frost, Melissa Knutson, and Ramatoulaye George-Alleyne developed and manage the book's Web site. Erika Paine, Michael Wishart, and Mauricio Abelo provided photos from the Bank's archives. Ms. Paine developed a holiday card based on the book. Angela Gentile-Blackwell, Phil Hay, Craig Hobbs, Andrew Kircher, Merrell Tuck, and Julius Wamy provided promotion support.

Marc Meadows, Heather Connelly, and the staff of the Meadows Design Office have shepherded the book through design and printing. A highly experienced book designer and producer, Marc is also an insightful reader. His comments improved the book greatly. Carla Langeveld prepared the bibliography.

The World Bank Office of the Publisher energetically supported the marketing of the book: Dirk Koehler, division chief; Jamila Abdelghani, Maya Brahmam, Stephenie DeKouadio, Alan Donovan, Connie Eysenck, Stacey Frank, Nicki Marrian, Randi Park, Hal Pollard, Don Reisman, Carlos Rossel, Carolyn Schiller, and Thaisa Tiglao.

It is also essential to mention the interest and encouragement of Jennifer Ruger of the president's office; Ian Newport and Christopher Lerner of the legal department; Veronique Danforth of the Info-Shop; Peter Easley, Sandy McDonald, Ben Moss, and Yuko Sunohara of the general services department; Michele Bailly, Valerie Chevalier, and Patrice Dufour of the Paris office; and Betty Hill, Nicole Kekeh, Rachel McColgan, and Nazanine Atabaki of external affairs.

The inspiration for this book comes from my husband and my children, Julia Spiegel and Spike Jonze. They, my mother, and our extended clan are a beacon to me.

Finally, I would like to cite Dominique La Pierre's *City of Joy*, a book that salutes the heroic struggles as well as the generosity and neighborliness of Calcutta slum dwellers living in the most desperate of circumstances. My aspiration is that, in some humble way this volume, too, will inspire admiration for the people in it and increase the commitment to eradicate poverty.

James D. Wolfensohn and the office of the president.

The external affairs, strategy and resource management, operations evaluation, poverty reduction and economic management, and general services departments; the South Asia region unit, the poverty reduction anchor, the World Bank Group Staff Association Executive Committee, and the Staff Association Poverty Working Group.

Sandra Granzow, task manager. Gita Hemphill, designer, coordinator of event. Karin Shipman, designer. Patricia Overend, team coordinator. Mauricio Abelo, Pelayo Alverez, Caroline Anstey, Alexandra Arenas, Salamata Bal, Namik Balci, Naye Bathily, Jamie Carvajal, Cynthia Casas, Beni Chibber-Rao, Andres Clerici, Luis Descaire, David Fischer, Rama George, Mary Hawkins, Betty Hill, Bonnie Howell, Kruti Kapadia, Gacangi Kiruthi, Seyda Kocer, Precinia Lizarondo, Beatrice Lopez, Jonathan Lyttle, Tchad Moore, Ian Newport, Joyce Petruzzelli, Deena Philage, Kevin Rafferty, John Randa, Rebeca Robboy, Javier Diez de Medina Romero, Kerry Saul, Katrine Saito, Gloria Martha Rubio Soto, Kalanidhi Subbarao, Carl Wessmann, Michael Wishart, Chuck Ziegler. Rachel Weaving, division chief, internal communications. Michael Walton, director, poverty reduction anchor. Jamil Sopher, 1998–99 chair, World Bank Group Staff Association.

Credits

QUOTATIONS USED AS EPIGRAPHS

Page 1: From "The Other Crisis," an address by James D. Wolfensohn to the World Bank board of governors, October 6, 1998.

LAND, FARMS, AND ROADS

India, page 16: Eric Newby, *Slowly Down the Ganges*. Penguin Books, 1966.

Morocco, page 26: Alfred A. Knopf, New York, *Morocco Guidebooks*. 1994.

REFORMING SCHOOLS, ENROLLING CHILDREN

Bangladesh, page 40: Tagore, Rabindranath. *Gitanjali*. New York: Scribner, 1997.

El Salvador, page 48: Alberto Masferrer. Use of quote authorized by Directoria Nacional de Promoción y Difusión Cultural.

THE STAFF OF LIFE

India, page 58: Words sung by Muniyammal, popular Indian singer.

Madagascar, page 68: Rossy. Madagascar. Compact disk. Lazer Productions, 1994.

Uganda, page 78: Peter Mattheissen, *The Tree Where Man was Born*. New York: Conde Nast, Penguin, 1972.

CITIZENS AS THE DOERS OF DEVELOPMENT

Benin, page 94: "To David Diop," a poem by Paulin Joachim, poet of Benin.

Mali, page 103: Ali Farka Toure with Ry Cooder. *Talking Timbuktu*. Compact disk, 1994. From the composition "Gomni" (Ali Farka Toure) Copyright © 1994, World Circuit Music Ltd. (PRS). All rights controlled and administered by Rykomusic, Inc. (ASCAP). Lyrics Used by Permission. All Rights Reserved. Embodied on the CD *Talking Timbuktu*, Hannibal Records HNCD 1381.

DOING GOOD WHILE DOING WELL

Estonia, page 120: John O'Brien, *Estonia— The Guide*. Tallinn: HUMA Publishing Ltd., 1993.

Bolivia, page 130: Gregorio Reynolds, "The Llama."

ONE NATION, TWO WORLDS

Argentina, page 138: Anthony Faiola, *Washington Post*, December 8, 1999.

HOLISTIC DEVELOPMENT ILLUSTRATED

Colombia, page 152: Internet report on 1999 human rights violations in the Madgdalena Medio, from the Colombia Support Network.

Colombia, page 154: *Los Angeles Times Magazine*, "The Cocaine Conundrum," September 24, 1995, Alan Weisman.

Vietnam, page 174: Pham Duy, Vietnamese Poet. Excerpt taken from song entitled, *Ti'nh Ca* or *Song of Love*.

ABOUT THE AUTHOR

Sandra Granzow divides her pursuits among journalism, communications, and development. She has worked on and written about development issues for the Asian Development Bank and the World Bank and produced television documentaries and programs for NBC, PBS, and USIA. She has a master's degree in foreign affairs from the Fletcher School of Law and Diplomacy and has consulted about development communications in Asia, Africa, and Latin America. She lives in Washington, D.C.

COLOPHON

The text of *Our Dream: A World Free of Poverty* was composed in Minion, a typeface designed in 1989 by Robert Slimbach for Adobe Systems Inc. Inspired by classical late Renaissance typography, Minion was designed specifically for current 20th and 21st century technology. It is appreciated for both its clarity and versatility, consisting of romans and italics with expert, alternate, and display characters.

This book was designed, typeset, and produced by Marc Alain Meadows on a Macintosh PowerBook G3 in QuarkXpress, and printed and bound in China by Everbest Printing Co.